Centered Living

The Way of Centering Prayer

M. Basil Pennington, O.C.S.O.

Foreword by Rabbi Lawrence Kushner

LIGUORI/TRIUMPH
LIGUORI, MISSOURI

Published by Liguori/Triumph
An imprint of Liguori Publications
Liguori, Missouri
http://www.liguori.org

Library of Congress Cataloging-in-Publication Data

Pennington, M. Basil
   Centered living : the way of centering prayer / M. Basil Pennington.
     p. cm.
   Includes bibliographical references.
   ISBN 0-7648-0495-2 (pbk.)
   1. Prayer—Christianity. 2. Contemplation. 3. Christian life—Catholic authors. I. Title.
BV210.2.P437 1999
248.3'2—dc21   99–30498

Printed in the United States of America
02 01 00 99 98 5 4 3 2 1
Revised Edition 1999

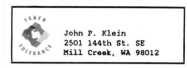

To Jeanette, Carl, Ferdinand,
and so many others
whose Centered lives are bearing
the rich fruit of compassion

Acknowledgments

M ost fundamentally I have to thank God, for all that I have is his most free and loving gift. All praise and thanks be to him. I want to thank my community, who create the context within which I am nurtured and supported. I want to thank all those who have allowed me to share Centering Prayer with them. It has been in the sharing and in the feedback that I have learned much. The best way to learn is to teach and to share. In particular I want to thank Franck, who helped me plan this volume and offered his challenging critique as each chapter developed, and Brother Anthony, who did the charts. And also those who offered their many suggestions in regard to the content: Mike, Phil, Georgieanna....

May the Lord reward you all as only he can.

Contents

Foreword to the New Edition

Rabbi Lawrence Kushner

Father Basil Pennington is a great, loving bear of a man. His laughter and embrace surround you with nurture. I have never known a man who was more gracefully centered within whom he was, within whom God had made him to be. And this pervades his writing on every level. We have the sense, reading his words, that they come from his *p'nimiyut*, his innermost essence. Indeed, in the volume before us we have a map for returning to our own innermost essence, our own center.

Perhaps the easiest way to begin to comprehend "centering" is to look at the world of creation all around us. Strewn everywhere, we encounter the presence of the Creator. And not merely in bluebirds and sunshine, but even in suffering and death, everywhere. This light is within everyone and everything and it yields itself to our focused gaze, our lightest touch. To find it is to revitalize ourselves and return us to our own root. But, of course, the experience of being centered is to realize paradoxically that there is no center at all. In such moments of contemplation the worshiper loses his or her sense of discrete boundaries.

My friend and teacher, Professor Daniel Matt (who is presently working on a twenty-year-long project to translate the Zohar, the master text of Kabbala), explains it this way in the following metaphor. Imagine a tree: leaves and twigs and branches and trunk and roots—a living organism in constant commerce with soil, wind, rain, and sunlight. We have words for each one of those things but just because we choose to give them names in our incessant drive to organize and control creation does not mean that the things themselves are discrete. The leaf, for instance, does not know when it stops becoming a leaf and becomes a twig and becomes a branch, nor does the branch know when it stops being a branch and becomes a trunk, nor the trunk roots, nor the roots the soil, nor the soil, nor the sky. All these names are only human superimpositions on the great organism of being itself. And to realize and acknowledge that we too are part of this great organism of being is to begin to find our own centers and understand why they are everywhere.

According to Hasidism, the eighteenth-century eastern European Jewish spiritual revival, such a momentary fusion with the divine is called *devekut. Devekut*, in Hebrew, means "to cleave." The worshiper no longer needs to talk *with* God because it is momentarily impossible to distinguish between the two: there is no worshiper, there's only God. It's all God! Individual needs and desires dissolve into the divine self.

Rabbi Yehiel Michel of Zlotchov, citing a teaching he heard from Rabbi Dov Baer of Mezritch in 1777, relates the following:

> ...and they yearn to make themselves one with the Holy One, likening themselves to nothingness (*ayin*). They understand that were it not for the power of the Creator who continuously creates and sustains them each moment, they would be nothing, just as they were before the creation. For indeed, there is nothing in the world except for God.
>
> It is just the opposite of what everyone else in the world thinks. They assume that when they do not merge with their Creator but cleave instead to the things and matters of this world, that they amount to something (*yesh*) in their own eyes. They imagine that they are important. But how could anyone who might not wake up the next morning be important? As we read

in Psalms (144:4), "Their days pass away like shadow," even while they're alive, it's all a show of vanity.

For this reason, if they think they are something (*yesh*), then alas, they are nothing (*ayin*). On the other hand, if, because of their fusion with the Creator, cleaving with all their physical and mental powers, they think of themselves as nothing, then they are very great indeed. They are like the branch of a tree that realizes it is part of one organic unity with its root. And the root, of course, is the One without end—the *Ayn Sof*, the One of Nothing. So, if the branch is one with the root and the root is the One of Nothing, then the branch too ceases to exist as an independent thing; it is nothing.

It's like a single drop of water fallen into the sea. It has returned to its source. It is one with the ocean. Now it's no longer possible to identify it as an independent thing in any way whatsoever.

In this way (and like all great spiritual metaphors) Centering Prayer can be seen as a way of understanding (and ultimately transcending) the relationship *between* each one of our individual selves and the One great Self of the Universe. As with virtually all Jewish teaching, this idea initially blossoms from the text of Scripture. Often, as in the following example, the insight grows from merely a seed, literally a dot or, in Hebrew, a *dagesh*. In Numbers 7:89 a very close reading of the Hebrew text reveals a fascinating irregularity. After all the princes of Israel have brought their gifts of consecration, Moses is left alone in the newly completed wilderness tabernacle.

The text reads: "[Moses] heard the Divine Voice speaking to him...." Given the context that does not seem especially noteworthy at all. But upon careful examination we notice one extraneous dot. Normally the Hebrew verb for "speaking, *mi-dabbaer*" appears in the *piel* conjugation and that requires a *dagesh* in the middle letter of the verbal root. But curiously here, in addition to the dot in the middle letter (*beit*), the first letter (*dalet*) is also vocalized with a *dagesh* of its own. And, that dot—according to all rules of Hebrew grammar—is *not* supposed to be there.

Turning to the commentary of Rabbi Shelomo Yitzhaki, (eleventh-century France) or, as he is commonly known by the initials of this name, Rashi, we learn the reason for the irregularity. Our verb, *midabaer*, says Rashi, is actually an odd form of what used to be *mitdabaer*, a *hitpael* conjugation form which used to include the letter *hey*. This letter *hey* has been assimilated so all that now remains of this swallowed letter *hey* is the *dagesh*!

We have solved the problem of the extra dot but replaced it with another one. Conjugation *hitpael* makes the verbal idea self-reflexive! This then renders our verse not "[Moses] heard the Divine Voice speaking to him," but reflexively: "[Moses] heard the Voice uttering itself." In other words, Moses overheard the Divine Self uttering itself! But if the Divine Self is uttering itself and the Divine Self is also the source of yourself then who is listening? We have come to the "center" of the Centering Prayer.

Did you ever talk to yourself? I don't mean when you were alone in the car. I mean did you ever ask yourself a question to find out if you knew the answer? Like, "Who am I?" or "What is the meaning of my life?" Did you ever get an answer? What would you do if the answer were "Who wants to know?" In other words, when you talk to yourself, who's talking and who's listening?

One of the discontents of civilization is the split between who we are and who is speaking. We are afflicted with a generic schizophrenia, disjunctive personalities. Call it the reflexive self: some *other* person who seems to be living *in there*. A piece of consciousness broken off from awareness. And the fact that we can hold these interior conversations with our "selves" means that we are fragmented, alienated, broken. If we were whole, then there could be no conversation, because there would be no one else *in there* to talk to.

I am convinced that such self-reflecting mind games are the enemy of religious experience. In the cinema, this is called "breaking the third wall," or alienation effect. The actor suddenly turns to the camera and speaks to it as if it were a real person, jarring the viewers into realizing they are only watching a movie. The spell is broken.

Rabbi Menahem Mendl Morgenstern of Kotzk (d. 1859) deliberately misreads the verse in Deuteronomy 5:5 in which Moses says, "I stood between God and you." Menahem Mendl teaches: it is your I, "your ego that stands between you and God. Normally not even an iron barrier can separate Israel from God, but self-preoccupation and ego will drive them apart."

My daughter once told me that the way to know I was dancing was to dance with so much of me that I stopped worrying about what I looked like on the dance floor. I told her that if she looked the way I did when I danced, she'd worry too. But she only said that in order to really dance, you must give yourself to the music. "Let it tell you what to do; quit being so self-conscious. The only way you will ever know you have danced, Daddy, is if, once the music has stopped, you realize you didn't know you were dancing."

This reminds me of a story told of Rabbi Hayim of Krosno. He once stopped with his students to watch a man dance on a rope strung high between two buildings. Rabbi Hayim became so absorbed in the spectacle that his disciples asked him what he found so fascinating in such a frivolous circus performance.

"I can't get over it," he explained. "This man is risking his life, and I am not sure why. I am sure that while he is walking on the rope, he cannot be thinking about the hundred gulden he is earning; he cannot be thinking about the step he has just taken or the step he is going to take next; he cannot even be thinking about where he is; if he did, he would fall to his death. He must be utterly unaware of himself!"

When we're dancing on the rope the inner conversation ceases. On reflection we realize that our sense of self is actually an obstacle. It splits us in two; renders us observers of our own lives; tricks us into thinking that our self is somehow other than who we are. There is only one of you in there and out here and it's the same one.

This loss of self and subsequent experience of unity is the touchstone of mysticism. As we have noted above, union with God in Judaism is called *devekut*. The classic sources are Deuteronomy 4:4: "But you that cleave unto the Lord your God this day are alive everyone of you this day." (The root letters for "cleave" are the same as those for *devekut*.) Also, the repitition of the word *anochi* in Isaiah 43:11, "I, I am the Lord," is understood to mean that the first I is God and the second is the self. Even Exodus 3:14, usually rendered, "I will be who I will be," now means, "I will be who you are!"

Those who seek the center don't want to just read about what God wants. We don't want someone else telling us what God wants either. We don't even want God telling us what God wants. We want our eyes to be God's eyes so that we can see the world the way God sees it. We want our teaching to be God's Torah. We want our hands to do God's work. We want our prayers to be God's prayers. We want to want what God wants. *Devekut*: being one with the Center!

Devekut, or *Unio Mystica*, gives us a new handle on a whole genre of statements that have always seemed both holy and heretical at the same time. For example, consider the following:

Rabbi Dov Baer of Mezritch advises his students: "...the best way to teach Torah is by not sensing oneself at all, being only instead as an ear listening to know how the world of speech speaks through you. You yourself are not the speaker. As soon as [you] begin to hear [your] own words, [you] should stop." The Baal Shem Tov, the progenitor of Hasidism, says: "When I fix my thoughts on the Creator, I let my mouth speak what it will, for the words are bound to the higher roots." Or Kalynomous Kalmish Shapiro of Piesetzna, who perished in the Warsaw Ghetto, explained that, "Not only does God hear our prayers, God prays them through us as well."

The Israeli scholar, Moshe Idel, in his *Kabbalah: New Perspectives*, identifies three different forms of *devekut* which precisely correspond to what I have long suspected were the three kinds of religious personalities.

Idel begins with what he calls Aristotelian *devekut*. I would call it cognitive *devekut*. In this form of union, during the act of cognition the knower and the known become one. Idel cites Rabbi Ezra of Gerona: "The ancient pious men caused their thought to ascend to the place of its source, and they would recite the *mitzvot* [commandments] and the [Ten] Commandments and through this recitation and this cleaving of thought...they received a [divine] influx from the annihilation of thought."

Here we have a description of the experience of the loss of self by a personality who is cerebral, rational, linear, left-brain dominant, someone whom we today might call a head person.

A second mode of *devekut*, Idel terms the theurgic. I would call it the *devekut* of behavior. In this experience, one seeks to literally affect God through specific actions. The *devekut* of behavior is predicated on the structural similarity and interdependence of the human body with the supernal image of God in the *Sefirot*. Rabbi Menahem Nahum of Chernobyl (d. 1787) teaches that "Commandment is called *mitzvah* because it joins together—punning on the Aramaic for *mitzvah* which is *tsavtah*, meaning 'team' or 'association'—the part of God that dwells within the person with the infinite God beyond. It may be, then...that [the *mitzvah*] contains the *shekhina* and in fulfilling it one has both [commandment and presence]."

In this mode of *devekut* your will, your deed, become God's. If one becomes a servant of God, then his or her action is God's action. By repairing things *here* we also repair them *above*. A personality drawn to such *devekut* is action oriented, content neither with study nor meditation; this personality is a doer, an achiever, a fixer, someone who wants to repair the world. If the first personality was a Head person, the second would be a Hands person.

The third and last form of *devekut* Idel associates with Neoplatonism. Its adherents are primarily concerned with the reuniting of the soul with its root. They draw heavily on the imagery of transformation, ascent, and return. I would call it the *devekut* of prayer. In describing this mode, Idel cites the work of an anonymous fourteenth-century Kabbalist: "The soul of the righteous one will ascend—while he is yet alive—higher and higher, to the place where the souls of the righteous [enjoy their] delight, which is the cleaving of the mind."

The focus of this third personality is neither cerebral nor behavioral but emotional instead. Such a soul is drawn to closing his eyes, loosing herself in song, sitting in silence. I would call such a one a Heart person. And thus, for each type of religious personality, becoming one with God finds its unique expression.

We can now reconsider the strange case of the extra *dagesh* in Numbers 7:89 and the question with which we began: how to stop being self-conscious. In the words of Nahman of Bratslav (d. 1811): "The core of a human being is his consciousness. Where one's consciousness is, there is the whole person. Thus one who knows and reaches an understanding of the divine is really in the divine. The greater one's knowing, the more fully is he included in his root in God."

Devekut is more than being *one with God. Devekut* is a theological metaphor for stopping the dialogue between the two inner voices. *Devekut* is a metaphor for self-unification. *Devekut* is a time when the outer person is revealed to be illusory, a figment of the language, an iron barrier separating us from God. Now only an unselfconscious awareness remains, an awareness that bears a wonderful similarity to the Divine. On *Yom Kippur* a woman in my congregation offered a personal prayer in which she prayed for the wisdom to "wish to be who she was."

Devekut is when the one who asks and the one who hears become the same. We realize to our embarrassment that we have been who we were all along and that it was only linguistic convention that tricked us into thinking we were someone else. We cannot make God do what we want but in thinking, doing, and praying what God wants, we become one with God and ourselves. I will be who you are, I even I.

This is also the center of the Centering Prayer.

L.K.
SUDBURY, MASSACHUSETTS,
MARCH 1999

Foreword

It was a crisp October morning at St. Joseph's Abbey in Spencer, Massachusetts. I was there on a retreat, one of many that I had made at the Abbey over the span of two decades. The custom for Mass at the Abbey for those attending the Eucharist is to place a host on the paten at the beginning of the offertory. Retreatants participating in the Eucharist are invited to join the offertory procession by Brother Francis. On that October morning Brother smiled at me as he invited me to join the procession. Tears came to my eyes as I walked behind Francis. There was something extraordinary about this monk. What was it? How is it that he communicated such sanctity without uttering a word? How is it that he needed no words to reveal so poignantly God's unconditional love for me?

Over the last twenty years I have visited many monasteries and convents in the United States, South America, Europe, and the Far East. In each of these monasteries I have observed and met monks and nuns who radiated a deep peace and joy, and who communicated incredible soul-nourishing wisdom and understanding.

There are people known to us all, such as Mother Teresa of Calcutta, who have done what seems like the impossible. In this book, among many others, you will read about Ferdinand Mahfood, who started Food for the Poor, and Deacon Carl Shelton, who started SHARE (Self-Help and Resource Exchange). As a result of Mother Teresa and her Missionaries of Charity, thousands of the sick and dying all over the world have been cared for and have died in peace and with dignity. Ferdinand's and Carl's ministries have resulted in millions who would have otherwise gone hungry receiving a daily meal. What empowers people like Mother Teresa, Ferdinand, Carl, and so many others to do such spectacular things for God?

More than twenty years ago Brother Jude responded to my knock on the Guest House door at St. Joseph's Abbey. I told Brother that I was going to take a course in the theology of prayer at The Catholic University of America and I would like some information on Centering Prayer. For me, at the time, Centering Prayer was not much more that a spirituality term. Brother asked if I would like to talk with Father Basil. I must say I was amazed that this was an option. My response was a wholehearted "You bet I would—is that possible?" A few minutes later a tall, bearded monk filled the doorway of the parlor where I was invited to wait. After explaining why I was there, Father Basil taught me Centering Prayer, centered with me, and answered my questions about the experience I had just had.

Thus started my experience with Centering Prayer. I regret to say that I was not always faithful to the advice of Father Basil, who became my spiritual father. I did not center every day and on the days I did, I did not always center twice. Over the years I had the good fortune of being in Father Basil's presence on numerous occasions. Whenever and wherever I was with Father we always centered twice a day for twenty minutes or longer each time. I remember centering with him and one of his Chinese friends and the friend's fiancée in a hotel lobby in Hong Kong. Another time Father and I were waiting for a ferry to take us from the Embarcadero in San Francisco to Alcatraz. Father found a bench on one of the docks and we centered while awaiting the departure of our ferry. And, we always centered during Mass after receiving the Eucharist. Now I am much more faithful to the practice as taught and regret that, unlike others, such as Brother Francis, Mother Teresa, Ferdinand Mahfood, and Carl Shelton that it took so long for me to respond in fullness to this ancient spiritual practice that enables us all to "be in faith and love to God who dwells in the center of our being." As Francis Thompson expressed so beautifully in *The Hound of Heaven,*

I fled Him, down the nights and down the days;
I fled Him, down the arches of the years;
I fled Him, down the labyrinthine ways
    of my own mind;
And in the midst of tears I hid from Him,
    and under running laughter.
Up vistaed hopes, I sped;
And shot, precipitated,
Adown Titanic glooms of chasmed fears,
From those strong Feet that followed, followed after.

The very fact that you have this book in your hands and are reading these words attests to the fact that God is inviting you into a deeper and more intimate personal relationship with him. This book may be your first exposure to Centering Prayer or you may have been engaged in this form of prayer for years and through this book will find the words to describe how you have been praying all along. Or maybe this book will be just the thing that will regain your attention; just the grace that will cause you to quit fleeing those "strong Feet" Francis Thompson heard in *The Hound of Heaven.* Or just the thing that will cause you to embrace wholeheartedly an ancient spiritual practice maintained and passed down through centuries. Father Basil Pennington, Father Thomas Keating, and Father William Meninger have been teaching Centering Prayer to the Church at large for the last thirty years in the hope that all might enter into the intimate relationship that God wants to have with each of us—each of us whom he continues to call forth in his creative love. Centering Prayer enables us to experience God and the fullness of who we are in God.

Aldous Huxley in *The Perennial Philosophy* said: "A society is good to the extent that it renders contemplation possible for its members; the existence of at least a minority of contemplatives is necessary for the well-being of any society." God invites us all to experience him in Centering Prayer. It is there that we will be drawn into the mystery of God and will be empowered to respond to the needs of God's human family.

In *Centered Living*, Father Basil grounds the reader in the rich historical background of Centering Prayer and teaches the seeker how to pray the prayer. Many accounts of how Centering Prayer has changed people's lives are related in the pages to follow, as well as how to support ourselves and others in the practice of Centering Prayer.

Plato said: "The human person's only hope of happiness lies in friendship with God." Flannery O'Conner said: "Eventually you have to grow religiously as in every other way, though some never do." You will discover in *Centered Living* the path to the friendship with God that leads to true happiness and a way to "grow religiously" into the fullness of who you are in God.

CAPT. MICHAEL T. MORAN, NC, USN (RET)

Preface

The Preface is a place for the author to say quite frankly why he wrote his book and what he hopes it will accomplish.

The why of this book is you. I have written this book because I love you. Just who you are I will say a bit more about in Chapter One. You are someone who has taken up Centering Prayer and made it a part of your life, of your journey into fuller life.

This book is also for you who have not yet learned or practiced Centering Prayer but feel a need for a deep prayer, a deeper, more experiential union with God. All the essential information about Centering Prayer will be found in this book.

If you are practicing another form of contemplative prayer this book may well enliven your prayer by contrast and complement. The applications to life will be fully relevant. For this reason, while the book as a whole will be especially helpful to anyone in ministry serving those who practice Centering Prayer, it will also be useful in a broader ministry.

There are three things I would like to do in this book. First of all, I would like to encourage you in your practice, perhaps answering questions that have come to mind, but more to strengthen your conviction of the value of the Prayer and your commitment to it. Then, I would like to offer you an opportunity to deepen your understanding of the Prayer. The second part of the book offers some theological reflections on the Prayer and its meaning in our lives—a kind of spiritual theology. The third part of the book is perhaps the most concrete in its practical proposals. It hopes to encourage and facilitate your sharing this Prayer with others. I find opportunities to share the Prayer almost every day. The hunger and thirst is everywhere. The cry is for teachers, even for spiritual mothers and fathers. May we be blessed with the courage to reach out and let the Lord make us fruitful.

I have written elsewhere about the three kinds of sacred reading that we need in our lives: *sacred study* to give understanding to the intellect, *motivational reading* to strengthen the will in its practice, and *lectio divina* to lead us into the experience of God. I hope this book will prove to be lectio for you—that it will open the space for you to experience God, who is with us as you listen to these words. The second part especially takes on the nature of sacred study, inviting you to a deeper understanding of your experience, of yourself and what happened to you at baptism, and of our God of immense love. Much in the book is meant to be motivational.

Some repetition will be found in this book, both within the text itself and in regard to my previous writings. I make no apology for this. The new context of both the teaching and the reader will make it a new experience. In Cistercian monasteries we call the talks the novice master gives to the novices three or four times a week "Repetitions." We need to hear basic things again and again, in different ways, from different angles. Repetition is the mother of wisdom.

Dionysios the Areopagite (actually this is the pseudonym of a fifth-century Syrian monk) speaks of three kinds of contemplation. There is the direct, which penetrates immediately into the depths of Reality. There is oblique contemplation, which reaches the Divine through the contemplation of the creation within which God hides and through which God can reveal Godself. And finally, there is circular contemplation. We, as it were, circle around the object and see it from many different angles, gradually being drawn into the fullness of its Reality. This book invites that kind of consideration. It seeks to circle around the subject, considering it from many angles, to lead the reader into a fuller appreciation of its inner Reality.

In reading this volume some may find the interweaving of

the very practical with the deeply theological a bit uncomfortable. Our rational mind wants to distinguish these things, sort them out, and organize data accordingly. But if we insist on always doing this in our minds, such compartmentalization may well carry over into our lives. This we do not want. We want to experience the fullness of theological Reality very practically in our everyday lives; we want it to flow through all we think and say and do. There needs to be a complete and constant interweaving of the two. This book, as a conversation close to life, allows this to happen.

If you have been practicing the Prayer regularly, you perhaps have no need of further motivation. The Prayer is, in many ways, its own reward. Yet, on this life's journey, we are all buffeted by many cares and concerns. Days get very full. Prayer can so easily get squeezed out. Undoubtedly, some of the asceticism connected with the Prayer lies in making time for it at the sacrifice of other good things. On the other hand, it sometimes happens that when we most have leisure for it—during vacation or during sickness—this unstructured time, which is a departure from our normal routine, lets regular practice slip away and we have a hard time recapturing it. We need to be motivated to keep coming back, even when God seems remarkable by absence.

I would never want it to be taken that I think Centering Prayer is the only or even necessarily the best way for each person to enter into the contemplative dimension of his or her life. I have seen beautiful persons become real contemplatives through the rosary and through other traditional practices and methods. I share Centering Prayer because it is very much a part of our tradition and it is the gift the Lord has given me. I believe that in its simplicity (I have tried in Chapter Four to simplify—and clarify—the method even more), it readily adapts itself to wherever one is on the journey. It can open the space for God to lead us all the way into the fullness of the life God offers us. It is a method that comes from our earliest Christian heritage. It has served Christians in all the intervening centuries. It is serving today in all parts of the Christian Community—geographically, sociologically, and hierarchically. It is truly a gift that belongs to all the People of God, for each one to use according to the particular leading of the Spirit, today, tomorrow, and unto the end.

I hope that you will hold me in your heart as you go to the Center, lest preaching to others I myself fall away. I promise you, my reader, my sister, my brother in the Lord, a place in my heart.

Free to Be Faithful

One day I had the privilege of participating in a sharing among a number of spiritual masters. Among them was the great Yogi, Swami Satchidanandaji. There was also an American professor who had become a very well-known and popular speaker on the spiritual journey. He had courageously stepped out of his secure university role in search of true wisdom and had spent time in India under a swami. He continued on his search and moved with each succeeding enthusiasm, leaving, insofar as he was able, no possibility untried. As our dialogue progressed and became more frank, open and personal, Swamiji turned to this teacher and said: "You are like a man who wants to find the living water. He digs three feet here, and three feet there, and three feet in another place, and so on. He never comes to the living water. You must stay in one place and dig deep. You must be faithful to one practice if you want to reach the living waters."

There are so many wonderful and rich methods of prayer in our fruitful twenty-century-old tradition. And we can draw on the wisdom of other traditions, also. What are we to do?

I believe those in ministry or preparing for ministry should seek some experiential knowledge of many different ways. They should know how to pray and from their experience know how to teach others how to pray in at least some of our traditional ways: the rosary, the Stations of the Cross, the breviary and other forms of liturgical prayer, the Jesus Prayer, Centering Prayer, Ignatian prayer, the Salesian method, and so on. They should also know experientially some of the possible contributive elements of other traditions, such as Yoga, Zen and insight meditation. But as life goes on, each of us needs to find the way that works for us and to practice it faithfully.

For most of us, community prayer will always be an important part of our lives. But we also need to go into our room and close the door and pray to our Father in secret. For this, each needs to find a practice that supports an increasing openness to God and an ever greater "yes" to his love.

If you have been introduced to Centering Prayer, that is not something that happened by chance. It was the Lord in his love who opened the way for you to receive this gift. True enough, it might not be the prayer for you at this time in your journey. Whenever I have conducted a Centering Prayer program, I have sought to remind the participants that their presence, a reality of God's grace working in their lives, is an invitation from him to enter into a deeper relation with him. I always urge that they practice the Prayer faithfully for a month or two and then reflect on their experience with the person who is accompanying them on the spiritual journey. If their previous way of praying was serving them better, then by all means they should return to it. If Centering Prayer was serving them better, then they should seek to be exquisitely faithful to it. Nothing is lost by such an experience, even if the decision is that Centering Prayer is not right for them now. Through their own experience they would come to understand something of the Prayer. They would be able to relate better with those who are practicing it. And they would be prepared for the day in the future when Centering Prayer would perhaps meet their evolving needs. Always the important thing is that we do spend time regularly with the Lord in deep, personal prayer, no matter what method or practice we use to support ourselves in doing this.

If you are one who has decided that Centering Prayer is the method for you, then I want to encourage you to practice it faithfully. I would like you to know that you are one of many, that your way of entering into the Prayer and your struggles with it are not uncommon. I hope that some clarifications, perhaps answering some of your own personal questions, will make your practice easier. While nagging questions can undermine our dedication, clarity can focus and strengthen it. If significant questions do remain for you, do get in touch with a Centering Prayer group, or attend a Centering Prayer workshop or retreat, or call or write a teacher. There are presently two web pages on Centering Prayer: <centeringprayer.org> and <centeringprayer.com> for the Contemplative Outreach as well as a number of discussion lists such as "centeringprayer" on <onelist.com>. Contemplative Outreach has a newsletter which you can receive by contacting them on the web or writing to:

Contemplative Outreach
10 Park Place Suite 2 B,
P.O. Box 737
Butler, NJ 07405

The prayer dimension of your life is extremely important and deserves some of your prime time, attention, and expense. Be good to yourself. Give priority where priority belongs. Dig your well steadily and deep so that you may rejoice in a life that is constantly nurtured by living water.

"We Are Legion"

I think it is good sometimes, when we sit down to begin our Centering Prayer, to take a moment to reflect that we are not alone. We are part of an immensely large community of brothers and sisters. Even as we sit apparently alone there are others, perhaps some quite near, others quite far away, who at the same moment are sitting with us before the Lord, or better, within the Lord. Grace and love flow from us, encircling the globe. The human family is embraced in a love that is of God. When we Center we are never alone. "We are legion." We are with many—many with whom we can rightly feel privileged to be, all one with our God of love in his healing and wholing of this earth of ours.

"We are legion." The text is right, but the context is off— for we are, by the mercy of God, on the side of the angels. We are, indeed, many, from all walks of life, rich and poor, young and old, lay and cleric, black and white and yellow, men, women, and children from dozens of nations, sons and daughters of both Covenants, and friends from afar.

Let me tell you about some of our "legion."

Centering Prayer has found its home and its fruit among the hierarchy; and it flourishes even more in the lives of the "lowerarchy." One of my favorite "success stories" is that of Dan, a blue-collar worker, who always affirms he knows no theology. (I immediately think of those words of Evagrius Ponticus: The man who prays is a theologian. The theologian is the man who prays.) Dan attended a Centering Prayer Retreat here at the Abbey. We always encourage everyone who learns Centering Prayer to begin immediately to share it with

6

others. Dan went home and asked his pastor if he could share it in his parish. Soon he was sharing it in neighboring parishes. Then he teamed up with sisters teaching in different retreat centers. He learned a bit about the "asanas"—yoga exercises—and took Centering Prayer to the YMCA as "Christian Yoga." And then to some high schools. He taught Centering Prayer at a soup kitchen on Skid Row and at the chancery of the archdiocese. The archbishop invited him to share it with the deacon class. The chief of police asked him to teach it to the rookies on the force before they hit the pavement to meet the tensions of a big city. Presently he is expanding his ministry into the prisons, caring for the men and women these police have arrested. In his teaching ministry (which he had to fit into his spare time, since Dan was still a full-time factory worker when he started teaching; now he is retired and can give himself more freely to his ministry) this young grandfather has elicited the support of his large family. As a married man, Dan knows his first call is to be a good husband and father. If the family can't see the fruits of Centering Prayer in his life, then he is missing the boat.

Centering Prayer is finding its place in the home and in the school. It is also finding a place in business. Some men find their office a good place to pray. Arriving a half hour early they sit at their desk and quietly Center before they start the day's work. Some have found a short period after lunch before tackling the afternoon to be far more helpful than the nap they used to take. (Take—that might be the key word. We stop taking and begin to receive. We will talk more about this later.)

One president invites all his employees to join him in Centering Prayer at the beginning of each business day. With his employees, he needs no argument. They all experience the benefits in a wonderful working environment and a dedicated, challenging, and compassionate boss.

Many married couples have shared with me the difference Centering Prayer made in the quality of their married and family life. They found a new depth and freedom in their being to each other in love and in the expressions of their love.

Gloria and Frank are an example of this. A middle-aged couple, they both had demanding professional responsibilities: Frank, as a therapist; Gloria, administering a large home health-care service. Their life, together and apart, has been full and rich. At the center of it all for them, both as a couple and as productive individuals, has been the time they Center together in the little meditation room they have created in their home. They happily shared their "secret" with all who would listen.

Indeed, now that Frank is retired he devotes much of his time to Contemplative Outreach.

Gregory is another beautiful husband, blessed with a most wonderful wife and five young children. Jayne and Greg know the importance of finding time alone together, and will go out to the fields and woods to watch the deer and see God. Greg is also enjoying an awakening relationship with his twelve-year-old son, Joshua, as well as contemplative moments with his younger ones. Greg writes:

> Contrary to popular opinion, contemplation is as appropriate in the home as in the monastery, in the living room as in the hermitage. The sacrament of marriage is an invitation to union—with spouse and with God. And contemplation is an adventure encountered by those caught up in love—a love which transcends both monastic rule and family routine. In both marriage and contemplation, beginners struggle in the absence of emotional highs. Overcoming this point of crisis in marriage or contemplation calls for complete fidelity— fidelity which leads to the heart of union and unconditional love. As the marital and contemplative relationship matures, devotion and fidelity become rooted in an unconditional love which transcends immediate gratifications and serves as a wellspring of intimacy and growth. Jayne and I realize that this intimacy and growth in our marriage are a source of support and encouragement toward our contemplative union. Contemplation has also provided a unique quality in our

relationships with the children....Younger children, too, can often be an inspiration in contemplation. They provide us, at times, with that extra incentive to seek the peacefulness of solitude. At other times, they offer us the example of loving simplicity—"for to such belongs the kingdom of heaven." Despite what seems to be a tendency of young children to chatter endlessly, they, too, have a need to appreciate the peacefulness of solitude. A few minutes of shared silence around a lighted candle can often be more meaningful, even to younger children, then several hours in front of the TV.... Finding time and space for solitude amidst the busy routines of family life presents a unique challenge. Despite this difficulty, Jayne and I have made detachment—detachment from care—a priority.

On the ecclesiastical side, there is that saintly man who was a true leader among the American hierarchy. I believe Cardinal Bernardin's witness was exceptionally beautiful and powerful. Let me quote what he wrote in 1983:

I came to understand that the pace of my life and the direction of my activity were unfocused, uncentered in a significant way. This created a certain unrest. I came to realize that I needed to make some changes in my life, and chief among these was a renewal of personal prayer. Mention of prayer may evoke an image of "saying" prayers, of reciting formulas. I mean something quite different. When we speak of the renewal of prayer in our lives, we are speaking of reconnecting ourselves with the larger mystery of life and of our common existence. This implies becoming disciplined in the use of our time, in the use of Centering Prayer, and in the development of a contemplative stance toward life. When this happens, we begin to experience healing, integration, wholeness, peacefulness. We begin to hear more clearly the echoes of the Word in our own lives, in our own hearts. And as that Word takes root in the depths of our being, it begins to grow and to transform the way we live. It affects our relationships with people around us and above all our relationship with the Lord. From this rootedness flow our energies, our ministry, our ways of loving. From this core we can proclaim the Lord Jesus and his Gospel not only with faith and conviction but also with love and compassion.

I think the Cardinal sums up well the process, the practice, and the fruits of Centering Prayer. All the Church would indeed rejoice to see such fruit in the lives of all our hierarchs!

When we first began consciously to share our contemplative prayer in our retreat house, our guests were largely priests and religious. Soon the Conference of Major Superiors of Men asked us to work with their membership, and the superiors of religious women joined in. The superiors, in their turn, brought the Prayer to their membership, and the members brought it into their ministry. In some instances new ministries and new centers were inaugurated.

Priests and sisters wrote back to us from the campuses. Students were looking for something besides the liturgy. The move east had peaked, as had also, in many instances, the charismatic movement. Serious students were looking for something quieter, deeper, to sustain them. Franck might be an example. A very gifted young man, he did exceptionally well in all he undertook. He would graduate with a 4.0 average, straight A's. He knew he could be distracted by the pursuit of excellence, good grades, interesting projects, a promising job, and lots of money. But in the end he would work through it all and be profoundly bored. He needed something more. He needed the challenge of a relationship with the Divine. Only God, with all his surprises, would be big enough for him. And for all of us, if we listen to our hearts. "Our hearts are made for you, O Lord, and they will not rest until they rest in you" (Saint Augustine).

Brothers write from high schools, where teenagers struggle

with the chaos of adolescence and find respite in the silence. Free from the structures they need to rebel against and the embarrassment of religiosity, they can be with God on their own terms.

One father shared this experience with me. As a Christmas gift he shared Centering Prayer with his teenage children. His older girls were excited about it and borrowed his tapes and books to teach their friends back at college. But Vin played it cool. As far as his dad could tell, no impression was made on his teenage son. Then, about six months later, Dad had occasion to go into Vin's room in search of something. He thought his son was away and barged in to find Vin sitting in meditation. When he questioned him about it later, Vin admitted he had been Centering regularly ever since his father shared the gift with him, but he didn't want anyone to think he was "religious."

The rector of my high school *alma mater* writes: "Each year the Juniors are introduced to Centering Prayer and clamor for more!"

The sisters tell me children are naturally contemplative. With a little encouragement and support they will prize and preserve that dimension of their lives. I have heard of one school where the whole student body sits together in meditation for twenty minutes at the end of the lunch break. The little ones seem to get easily caught up in the overall climate of prayer. The sisters say it is a good investment of school time because of the remarkable improvement in discipline, conduct, and even grades.

One sixth-grade teacher begins each day with twenty minutes of Centering Prayer. If it is omitted because of an assembly or Mass, the students pester her until she makes time for it. On Monday, the students check each other out: "Did you meditate on Saturday and Sunday?"

How young are our youngest meditators? A mother shared this with me: While she gets breakfast ready, her husband and the five children who will be going off to school sit and meditate together. Once they are all out the door, her three-year-old runs to his meditation chair. The two of them sit in prayer together for twenty minutes and then they play together for a bit. Talking to her little one, the mother is certain he is having beautiful experiences of his heavenly Father's love.

Centering Prayer has also touched the crowned heads of nations. The king and queen of a European country were taught by a married deacon from the United States. This prosperous businessman's heart was turned to the poor after he began Centering (I'll tell you more about him later), and in God's wonderful, paradoxical way, he soon found himself consorting with the very rich.

There is a flourishing Centering Prayer group among the retinue of one of the Third World dictators. Unfortunately the dictator himself has not yet joined the group, but when he does—we can pray for that—I am sure we will see great changes in that sorely tried nation.

It would not be possible to list all the vocations and professions to be found among those who have made Centering Prayer their way of grounding their lives. Just a random look through the many letters in my files turns up an Episcopal priest, a doctoral candidate, a spiritual director, a retired sister, a probation officer, a psychiatric nurse, an abbot, a teacher, a Jewish rabbi, a sister in parish ministry, an employment counselor, a book reviewer, a woman in hospice work, a Roman Catholic archbishop, a Trappist monk, a wife and mother, a hospital chaplain, a model, a housewife who signs herself a "good Protestant," a retired commercial airplane salesman, a mother who is a lay apostle, a CCD teacher, a parish organist from Ireland, a missionary, a director of a retreat center, a student nurse, a provincial superior, a research fellow at Yale, a Benedictine abbot from Brazil, a medical doctor, a swami from India, a college chaplain, a Benedictine oblate, an Anglican bishop, a single mother managing a business employing one hundred, a schoolteacher in Pakistan, a semiretired principal (who can see an entirely new ministry in answering the plea of so many, an echo of the apostles' "Teach me how to pray"), a cook from Ireland, a prison chaplain, a Maryknoller, a theology student in Rome, a Marist missionary sister, the Father General of a religious order, a rector of a seminary, a married couple, a sister in India, "a part-time moonlighting writer," an elementary schoolteacher in Edinburgh, a receptionist at Catholic Worker, a secretary, a man who has "a blue-collar job and spend[s] much more time writing," an Anglican nun in England, the prior of a Charterhouse, a Franciscan novice and a Redemptorist novice, a deacon, a public-school administrator, a laboratory technician (who left her job—connected with making the guidance system for the Trident and MX—after four months of Centering Prayer), a professor of psychology, and a housekeeper for a parish priest in New Zealand.

I am touched by the openness of the many who write, their eagerness to share something of their journey. Centering Prayer has entered lives at very different points on that journey: "My 42 years as a nun...," "49 years of teaching, nearly four years in retirement...," "I am 34...," "I am retiring in a few years...,"

"Being a brother of 54, and having finished teaching after 34 years in class...," "I am a theology student...," "I am a North American Daughter of Charity, 63 years old, about 45 years vocation...," "I am a retired teacher, 78 years old, and act as receptionist and secretary...," "I am a Dutch Oblate missionary here in Haiti, 55 years old...," "I feel perpetually youthful (I'm 44) and don't fear aging...," "I am a novice...," "I am 81 years old...," "I am 47 years of age, have been a priest for 21 years...," "I am a 41-year-old woman...," "As a priest who looks forward to celebrating my thirtieth anniversary of ordination at Michaelmas...," "I go off to college in the Fall...."

There is hardly a day when I do not hear from someone who has a story to tell about what Centering Prayer is doing in his or her life, or someone looking for what Centering can provide. Today, it was an exceptionally gifted and sensitive young man from a Catholic Worker farm; he shared how important was the silent time to meet the challenges of community life and open hospitality. Yesterday, Dan called to ask our prayerful support; this weekend he will be responding to a request from a group of divorced and separated Catholics who want to learn Centering Prayer. Last week my nephew drove me to the airport; we talked about the tensions he was experiencing, breaking into the business world, working for a master's degree in business administration and coming to terms with family and social relations. He very much wants to find that Center from which he can draw the peace, confidence, and strength he needs.

And what of the sick? Mom—as I always called my friend's mother—had terminal cancer. As she lay in bed she gently complained she could no longer pray. She couldn't hold the little book she had so long used. The old formulas just dried up. Even the rosary didn't seem to work. Gently, I told her how to Center in her heart. A new peace and joy filled her life.

I remember very especially Sister Penelope—everybody called her Penny. Sister was part of a parish team. They had taken me in for the night and soon we were sharing Centering Prayer. As we came out of the first experience, I looked around. I saw a beautiful smile on Penny's face. "You must have had a good experience," I said. Sister then told me she was dying of bone cancer. This was the first time in months she had been able to leave her pain behind. When I visited her in the hospital five months later, not long before her death, sister again expressed her gratitude for the gift of Centering Prayer. It had turned the painful months into the beginning of heaven on earth for her. I have always believed that it was because of her contemplative prayer during those months that her parish became a Centered parish. They never begin a service or a meeting without spending some time in Centering Prayer. We certainly have our patron saints of Centering in heaven. And I am sure they are still, in their own most special way, Centering with us.

Not only the physically afflicted find a way in this Prayer. Sister Anna Polcino, the founder of the House of Affirmation, believes strongly in its healing power for those who are afflicted with deeper wounds. I have, on a number of occasions, had the privilege of sharing the Prayer with priests and religious at the House. Sometimes the only way we can pray is to be with the Lord in our pain and let that groan be before him. In yesterday's mail I received a letter from a priest at a medical facility for alcoholic priests where Centering Prayer is part of the daily program. He witnesses to the same experience. An Indian Jesuit who has been teaching Centering Prayer since 1981 writes from Bombay: "I have seen many persons getting cured of their psychological problems. Where counseling failed this method worked."

Yes, "We are legion." And yet we are one. We will talk later about the full Reality of this oneness. For now we can note our common qualities.

Courage is one of them. We have to have courage to face our own loneliness and need rather than hiding it behind some false self. And knowing from our own hunger—as well as, perhaps, from the witness of others—that there has to be something more, we courageously step out in search of it. We are willing to let go of the unsatisfying "false self" and risk new spaces—spaces in which God can show up.

Centering Prayer is for those who want more—infinitely more. It is for those who dare to believe that they are made to be intimate with God and the bearers of his life and love in this world. It is for those who truly love themselves, love themselves enough to put first things first: to give God his time, to give themselves this time in God, so that they can give to others quality time that is loving and creative.

How Did We Get Here?

How did we get here?—to this place at the Center?—to this union with God and with everyone else at the Center? Or perhaps I should more properly ask: How do we get here? For it is an unending process; it involves a constant choice to be at the Center, to be in touch with our deepest being, the ground of our being—to be in touch with reality as it truly is.

People have been introduced to Centering Prayer in many different ways. For some it was through an article or a book, or through a workshop or a retreat or an evening lecture. Some have listened to tapes or a television show or a radio talk show. Some have learned it from a friend or it was the practice in their home. Some have learned it in the classroom or at lectures offered by the chaplaincy.

And some have come to it quite naturally, as it were. Almost always when I speak about the Prayer to an elderly group, one or another will say: "Oh, I have been doing that for years."

I first came to it myself quite naturally (if that is the word— obviously we come to this only by the grace of God; it is something quite beyond us, essentially supernatural, yet sometimes it seems quite natural as our relationship with the Lord evolves). When I was in high school I used to help out in CCD and CYO in a tough inner-city parish. When evening came, I was often well played out and quite frustrated. We seemed to accomplish so little. I would go into the church and just be with the Lord and let my weariness and pain be before him. His name would rise up from my heart from time to time, intensifying our togetherness. It was as simple as that.

16

It was on the trolley car that I first began to realize the significance of the transformation that was taking place. It was always a painful thing for me to ride on the trolley. I was sensitive to the faces around me, so many of them set in pain. I longed to do something, but sat there impotent. Then one day I realized I had God in me, the fullness of divine, creative Love. And I began to pour out that Love on those around me. I could see a change come into faces. Sometimes people even looked up and smiled at me. And on rare occasions, as they passed me leaving the car, they would murmur, "Thank you." Instead of leaving the trolley weighed down by my impotence, I got off refreshed, invigorated by the Love that had been flowing through me. There were no fireworks, just a quiet sense of an empowering Love that cherished and affirmed me and was a Gift that I could give to others.

When I entered the novitiate the novice master assumed we were all beginners in prayer who had to go through all the steps and stages. A fairly standard manual was placed in our hands to help us learn all about discursive meditation. I found the latter impossible, at least as prayer. It could be an enjoyable mental exercise. I like to think things through and use my imagination; but for me this was no way to pray, to be with God. I went to the abbot with my frustration. He asked me how I did pray. When I told him I just sat there with the Lord and used his name to be attentive to him in love, the abbot assured me that the way I had found or been led into was a quite valid traditional way of prayer. He encouraged me to persevere in it.

As Greg pointed out in his letter which I quoted in the last chapter, there is a close similarity between marriage and prayer. God himself seemed to find marriage his favorite image when he tried to express to his people, to you and to me, the kind of relationship he wants with us. Read again the Song of Songs, the Book of the Prophecies of Hosea, or some of the other prophets. Saint Paul brought this revelation over into the New Testament. It is really the story of any growing, deepening relation. As it deepens, words become less and less useful. They begin to get in the way. We simply want to be with each other, to each other, without ideas, or thoughts, or projects getting in the way.

In this regard, for some, learning Centering Prayer has been a real breakthrough. They had been faithful for years to methods of prayer learned in earlier days. But they longed more and more for something else. One lay woman wrote:

> How I wish I had had something like this years ago as I was taught that the type of prayer you write about was obtainable only after years of vocal prayer and meditation—the "what does it mean–what does it mean to me–what am I going to do about it" method. The resolution, remote preparation, immediate preparation, and the details entailed in this often proved a burden and a distraction when I longed only to kneel in silent prayer and adoration.

This woman learned of the Prayer when she found a copy of *Centering Prayer* in her local public library.

We will speak later about the preparation necessary for one to fruitfully enter into Centering Prayer. There is still, especially among religious and others who have read much about prayer, a certain amount of fear in regard to a contemplative type of prayer. A sister in Pakistan, who learned the prayer from my tapes and had been practicing for a short time, wrote of her fears: "I felt this type of prayer was an answer to what I have felt a need of for some time.... I intend asking the Lord about this need and feel he will supply in due time, but for now I do not want to continue and fool myself into a pseudo-mysticism or simply find myself looking for a 'high' in prayer. All in all, it is a pleasurable experience and I wonder if I could not get lost in seeking the pleasure and not the dark silence where dwells the Lord."

It is a humble fear, but one that is unfortunately grounded oftentimes in false notions drawn from systematic treatments of the "spiritual life." These plot out the way carefully with all the steps and stages clearly marked. The many possible pitfalls are amply described and proud presumption is underlined as the most nefarious of them all. What has all this to do with the simplicity of the gospels? "Come to me all you who labor and are heavily burdened [with many conceptualizations] and I will refresh you" And with their call to intimacy: "I would as a mother hen gather you under my wings....I will come in and sup with you; we will sit side by side"? We need not fear to be with the Friend as a friend, if only we want truly to be his friend. Our sins are no obstacles so long as we do not cling to them but rather let them go and let his saving grace take care of them as we turn to him.

For many in the charismatic movement, Centering Prayer has been not so much a breakthrough as a natural evolution. As their affective prayer grew, they experienced the need to complement it with some quieter, deeper prayer. As meetings have matured, more spaces are left for silence. Some meetings provide regular opportunities to learn Centering Prayer.

For many, Centering Prayer has been a return. In a search for that wholeness which is in truth holiness, they set out toward the East. It was a familiar pattern. It has reoccurred whenever the local synagogue or church has failed to bring the fullness of its heritage to its daily ministry. Young hearts in moments of grace seek for the fullness that is rightly theirs to seek. And when it is not to be found at home, they courageously go forth in search of it. The Lord loves this. When the fishermen from the shores of the Sea of Galilee went east across the Jordan in search of something more, he rewarded their search with the true Find and constituted them leaders of the people who would hear his word: Seek and you shall find. My own patron, Saint Basil, Father of the monks of Eastern Christendom, left the schoolrooms of Athens with his friend Gregory and headed east. So did John Cassian and Paula and others from Rome. And so on through the centuries. In our time we have seen the searchers go forth from the shores of America to India and Japan. They went forth in such numbers that the masters themselves were drawn to come from the East.

In looking to the East there are some things we have to keep in mind. We Christians are the privileged sons and daughters of the Revelation, receiving it in a fullness even beyond that of Abraham, Isaac, and Jacob and the great Moses. "Prophets have longed to see what you see and have not seen it, to hear what you hear and have not heard it....I no longer call you servants but friends because I have made known to you all that the Father has made known to me." We have to be profoundly humble in this, for the sad truth is that many who have received less have done more. It will be they who will receive the praise of the one who appreciated the widow's mite. Yet the fact remains, one who has been baptized into Christ has been made a partaker of his very nature and life. We can never hope to attain fullness and integration outside of Christ, no matter how enlightened a master we might choose. Indeed the more enlightened masters always encourage the seeker to be true to his or her own tradition, to bring whatever one finds in the master's teaching back to the fuller living of one's own native path.

Many who have honestly gone forth in their search have come to recognize the reality of this. And for many of them Centering Prayer has been the way back. It has opened their eyes to the light of their own tradition—which has, alas, been hidden under a bushel basket for a long time. Well prepared by ascetic and faithful practice, they enter quickly and deeply into Centering Prayer and find that Love for which they are made and for whom they have been longing.

Others, perhaps more prudent or less courageous, or perhaps bound more by the structures of their youth, have watched these seekers go forth and have envied what they were finding. Yet they themselves did not want to go forth from their own tradition. Christians of many different communions have refound this rich vein of our common Christian heritage through Centering Prayer and have been delighted to reclaim it. A priest writes of a clergy retreat where an Episcopal abbot teaches Centering Prayer. A woman writes from England at the behest of an Anglican bishop. A man concludes his letter: "I am a

Moravian. I do not write that defensively but because we have lost this part of our tradition." It is good to find it again, and to be able to do that without having to leave the fullness of one's own Christian heritage.

By far most have come to Centering Prayer out of an experienced need. That is the way I came to it, and my nephew, and Franck, and Cardinal Bernardin. Our experienced needs were different. But in the end they are the basic and most profound needs of the human heart—the need for God, the need for the infinite, for a compassion, a strength, a challenge big enough to call us forth in all our fullness, a meaning big enough to make it worth carrying the world in our hearts with infinitely tender care—a love that really makes a difference.

It may begin, as it did with me, with just the need to find the strength to manage the drudgery, the pain, the frustrations of each day. Or it may come from an insight into the ultimate boring delusion of all that this world has to offer to fill the human heart. Or it may crash in, as we are suddenly confronted with a terrible lack of fulfillment after years of life and labor. There has to be something more! And Centering Prayer says, "Yes, there is." Beneath all our feelings, beneath our reasoning, beneath all our limitations, there is a deep Center, the Center and ground of our being, and we can pass through that Center into the very Center of God. Indeed, the two Centers are one—constituting the very Center of all that is. It is the creative Source, who can fulfill all our deepest and broadest and loftiest aspirations. And more, for "eye has not seen, nor ear heard, nor has it entered into the human heart what God has prepared for those who love him."

And, finally, among the seekers finding their way into Centering Prayer are those who have become the mature children fit to enter the kingdom of heaven. Without long journeys, courageous searching, or deeply felt need, they have been simply open to the unexpected invitation of the Lord and have entered in. Happy are they, for they have learned from within the pattern of the Divine instead of having had to struggle with the fragments of a badly fractured world.

Whatever path has led us to Centering Prayer, it is only a beginning. And that, of course, is part of the excitement of it. There is no end. Those words of the psalmist become very much our own: "I thank you, God, for the wonder of my being—not to speak of the wonder of your Being." We will never be bored.

But for each, the journey is different.

For some the first steps in Centering Prayer are wonderful. A student at Catholic University writes: "Learning Centering Prayer was one of the biggest moments of my spiritual life.... You changed my prayer life and indeed my whole life that day. I have stayed with the Centering Prayer ever since with great results." He is a fortunate young man, perhaps one of the "little ones" who has entered readily into the kingdom. Or perhaps a weak one whom the Lord is alluring with consolations, as Jesus first showed himself to Peter, James, and John on Tabor in great brightness and clarity before the cloud came over them and they were filled with great fear.

Most, when they first began to Center, experienced some of the usual natural concomitant benefits—the release of tension, some peace and repose—and some sense of God. But the Prayer for the most part was darksome. They were entering the cloud of unknowing.

For others the first steps seem to be filled only with struggle. They go on only because of their need and because no better hope is held out to them by any other path. They trust a teacher, a friend, others who proclaim the benefits of Centering Prayer. They do have a hope—a beautiful gift from the Lord. They go on. And then there is a breakthrough. A forty-four-year-old lay woman writes:

> The first four months of Centering Prayer were, in my personal experience, very dry and unfulfilling, but I persevered because I knew that I would find God that way. I found it to be excruciating not to be able to "do" something, and my mind kept chasing mental butterflies. I shared this experience of learning Cen-

tering Prayer with my very good friend, so I had someone to discuss it with. Finally, after about four months,
I experienced the Center and knew that everything
was different, that I would never be the person I
was before that happened to me. It gets better all
the time, and it's such an amazing thought that God
would take the time with me to do repair work in my
soul. I know that I have experienced the kingdom of
God within me, that I have already "passed from death
to life" and that eternal life is knowing God. Best of
all, I know that through Centering God renews me
daily....

A housekeeper in New Zealand had a similar experience:

You may remember I wrote to you last year that I had
read your book on Centering Prayer....For a long time
I found it very difficult to switch off everything and
concentrate on him even with the Prayer word. But in
the last month I have had tremendous breakthroughs
in many areas, and I can now get close to the Lord
without fear being involved, and also open to his love,
complete and unconditional and free—no strings attached—maybe just one, to love him. Now this Centering Prayer has become very real, very deep....It is
Good Friday today and I went round to the church to
just sit and center. Things have "come alive" in me
about the Passion, Sufferings, Death, and Resurrection for the first time. This morning I didn't want to
stop centering but had to before I burst with it all.

But sometimes the darkness just seems to go on and on,
and nothing happens. One of our abbots told me of a young
religious who was having such an experience. In his community they all Center together for half an hour after the early
morning prayer. This young man came to the abbot repeatedly, complaining about the Prayer. It was, he said, two min-

utes of prayer and twenty-eight minutes of spaghetti. He wanted to have permission to leave the meditation group and go do some Scripture prayer on his own. Finally, the abbot gave in, in spite of his own judgment that the young man was in fact showing the fruits of the Prayer in his life. After a relatively short time the young man was back to the abbot, repeatedly confessing outbursts of anger, uncharitableness, and unkindness. He was beginning to feel depressed. Some of the joy had seeped out of his life. The abbot made bold to suggest: "Maybe those twenty-eight minutes of spaghetti were nourishing you after all."

Of course, the young man's judgment was off on a number of counts. First of all, Centering Prayer is all prayer, even when we are beset with thoughts, provided we are faithful in following the practice and continually return to the Lord each time we become aware that we are being drawn away. There were undoubtedly many acts of love in this young man's prayer as he repeatedly returned to the Lord. He had forgotten that we cannot judge the Prayer in itself. The times we are drawn out by thoughts, we can remember. But that is all we can remember. The time we are in the Presence takes us beyond time and the realm of those things we can remember. If we try to judge the Prayer by what we can remember we are apt to make the same judgment this young religious made: it was mostly spaghetti—mostly thoughts. The contrary might very well have been the case. Another fact is that we ourselves sometimes are the last to see the fruits in our lives. Our Lord gave us several parables about the subtleness of spiritual growth. Others usually see and experience the change in us, the fruit of the Prayer in our lives, long before we do.

Most who are faithful to the Prayer have experienced that after a time the inner eye does adapt itself to the deifying light. They begin to see things differently, to experience life in another way. I will talk more about this in the next chapter. I often liken this experience to attending a matinee. Have you ever gone to the movies on a bright sunny day? We sit in the theater for several hours watching the images on the screen.

Our eyes totally adapt themselves to these unrealities and see them as real. Then, when the show is over, we step out into the brilliant sunlight. What is our first experience? All is black. Our eyes cannot take in the true light with all its brightness. Happily, our eyes quickly adapt themselves. Then we see the real world with great clarity in the bright light of the sun.

We have been used to seeing only the surface of things. There is a certain unreality in this. We see things as if they existed in themselves. In reality, they exist because God is there every moment, sharing with them something of his very own being, goodness, and beauty. If we really see things and persons, we also always see God. When we first turn our attention in faith to God dwelling in the depths of our being, because we have so little used our eyes of faith illuminated by the gifts of the Spirit, they are poorly adapted and can only experience a certain darkness. It takes time, leaving the surface images and concepts behind, for the inner eye and ear to adapt to the all-pervasive radiance of the Divine Light and the celestial harmonies.

As I have indicated above, it usually happens that those who do enjoy great sweetness and light in the first days of Centering Prayer are later led into the cloud of unknowing. Indeed, for almost everyone there are alternations. We have days and seasons of light and experienced Presence and then times when the dark clouds do roll in. This really doesn't matter at the deepest level. We go to the Prayer to give ourselves to God—drawn by him, or we would not go—and the light and the dark are secondary. If we truly love, we respect those we love and let them be themselves. In our love, we let God be to us the way he wants to be. Knowing his love, we can be certain he is being to us in the way that is truly best for us at this time. If he hides in the cloud it is only to increase our desire, so that he might give himself to us ever more (read again the Song of Songs). God does love us and respect us. He will never force himself on us. He gives himself to us only insofar as we want him. Therefore the important thing is that our desire for him continually grows. Both his absence and his presence can cause our desire to grow. He will give us whichever he knows will best help us at this point in our journey. Such is his great love.

There really are no rules, nor should we try to set rules or expectations as to how our experience in Centering Prayer should evolve. It is a relationship between two unique persons, each with his or her own freedom. The Lord is going to respond to each of us freely and uniquely. And we want to respect fully his freedom to do that. For our part, we want to be faithful, open, respectful, and above all loving—self-giving and totally available to his love.

I have a friend in the monastery, to me a very special person. We like to get together each day for a cup of coffee. When we miss this get-together we miss it. Some days he has a lot to say, some days I do, some days we both do. Some days neither of us does, and we just sort of sit there together. This get-together is important. Yet I never go away from it wondering if I did it right today. We just do it, and enjoy it. Centering is my "coffee break" with the Lord. That, simply that—and much more.

When we have an ongoing relationship with someone, especially a long-standing one, we don't constantly examine it to see how it is going. It is a fact in our lives. It is something we choose. And we have to keep on choosing it, in the sense of giving it time and energy and its due priority. Any good relationship will have its fruits or benefits, its rewards if you will. We may be more or less conscious of them. We may or may not be particularly aware of them as flowing from the relationship. The fruits are there, but we are usually more directly concerned with the relationship itself.

I get a lot of feedback from those who read my books, listen to my tapes, attend my lectures and workshops. They see the fruits of Centering Prayer in my life and in the way I am to others. I usually don't think too much about all this. When I hear them, I thank God for what he is doing. But I am concerned about the one essential: union with God, allowing him to use my life the way he wants for his glory and for the good of the whole human family. The last time I was with

Mother Teresa in Calcutta I asked her for a word for my community. She replied: "Ask them to pray that I do not get in God's way." That is my concern. I know I need Centering Prayer to keep the channels clear, to keep the reservoir full and overflowing. I need it to keep me honest and free from self-deception. I need it to keep me from yielding to discouragement as I see my constant failures, my great needs, the great needs of others, and my inability to respond. I need regular Centering Prayer so that God can shine through my life. But when I go to Center I don't think about all this. I go because I want to spend the time with the Lord, my Friend, my Lover, my God.

Each of us has his or her values, needs, and priorities. Some will be more conscious than others of the fruits they hope to reap from meeting the Lord at the Center. Greg and Jayne seek detachment—detachment from cares. Franck seeks a challenge in the relationship—one big enough to give meaning to the rest of his life. Many seek just that, the key to the meaning of their lives. For some, that means peace. Others call it hope. These are all fruits of Centering Prayer and we need to talk more about them. For they are part of our being here, where we are right now; part of the reason we have gotten here; and something that will motivate us to keep on going, to be ever more faithful in meeting the Lord at the Center and letting him bring about in us, in all its fullness, that transformation of consciousness that will enable us to live constantly out of the Center.

The Untold Fruits
of Centering Prayer

I regularly receive letters which say, for example: "Then I began to practice Centering once a day. And with quite amazing results in my life!" and "My whole spiritual life has been revolutionized and it has flowed into everyday happenings," and "I meditate at least twice a day for at least twenty minutes each time. It is the most important part of the day. It is the most important part of my life." What makes people write things like this? What are they getting out of Centering Prayer that makes such a difference in their lives?

Before I begin to share with you what I myself and what others are receiving from Centering Prayer—the benefits, the rewards, the fruits of the Prayer in our lives—I would like to make a suggestion. I would like to recommend that you take a couple of minutes, or longer if you wish and find it fruitful, and consider what you want to get out of life. What is missing? What is that something more that you would like to have—perhaps quite undefinable but nonetheless sensed? We all want happiness. But happiness consists in knowing what we want and then knowing we have it or are on the way to getting it.

Take a little time, perhaps with pen in hand. Pray. Ask the help of the Spirit. Listen to the depths of your own heart. There is so much frustration in life because we don't listen to our own heart and its deep longing. We don't make time for ourselves, to hear ourselves and care for ourselves. Be good to yourself and give yourself a bit of time. What do you want?

$\sim$

The first thing we receive from Centering Prayer, indeed the very essence of it, is God himself. Perhaps that is not precisely accurate. God is, of course, the very essence of the Prayer; but he is already present, given to us. He is ever with us as our Creator, bringing us into existence by sharing with us something of his goodness, life, and being—a sharing brought to a new fullness through the grace of baptism. This is a fact. And we know this by faith. What happens in Centering Prayer is that we come to know this by experience. We know that God is truly with us, an affirming, loving Presence. Yet it is a new kind of knowing. It is a sense that gently and effectively pervades our whole being. It leaves us with a good feeling about the Prayer, even when the Prayer has seemed but emptiness and darkness. It is a sense that gradually pervades our whole life. God is with us. We are never alone. The consciousness surfaces constantly and spontaneously.

This is a very integrating and therefore a very satisfying experience. What has been a fact in reality, that God is with us, we now come to know, and not just intellectually but affectively and experientially. This fulfills the aspiration of the human mind and heart. We are made with an infinite capacity to know and to love. "Our hearts are made for you, O Lord, and they will not rest until they rest in you" (Saint Augustine). In the moments of transcendence in the Prayer this is complete. Afterward there is a certain sense of it, a certain peace and joy. We know that the deep aspirations, the longings and emptiness can be filled. We are not destined to live in frustration. A great philosopher, Plato, in one of his writings comes to the true conclusion that the human person's only hope for happiness lies in friendship with God. But then this great seeker, who had not yet received what we have so undeservedly received in the Revelation, cries out in deepest frustration: "But this is impossible." For us of ourselves it is impossible; but all things are possible with God.

For many of us the most intense moment of communion with God prior to Centering has been a moment of Holy Communion—those special Communions when he was so very present. I was struck this afternoon when a priest said to me that for him Centering Prayer was holy Communion. I remembered what one of our twelfth-century Cistercian Fathers, William of St. Thierry, said of the moments when the monk is in his cell enjoying this kind of prayer:

> For both in a church and in a cell the things of God are practiced, but more constantly in the cell. In a church, at certain times the sacraments of Christian religion are dispensed visibly and in figure. In cells, as in heaven, the reality which underlies all the sacraments of our faith is constantly celebrated. And they are celebrated with as much truth and in the same order as they are in eternity, although not yet with the same untarnished magnificence or the same security.

In this experience of union we come to know God in a new way. We know in whom we have believed, as Saint Paul puts it. "Taste and see that the Lord is good." God is no longer just someone we read about, or hear about. He is as real to us as the taste of an orange. We know him. And we know that he is good, and good to us. The effect this has on our whole life of prayer, worship, liturgy, and sacramental encounter is transforming.

For most of us, most of the time, God is known in the cloud of unknowing. We know and we don't know. We know; our whole being senses it. But we don't know; we can't define it. We can't speak of our experience in any truly coherent way (hence the stumbling of all this writing). And yet, at moments, shafts of light do break through. Moments of awe, when our whole being says: "Yes, God, glory." We stammer, and our words have infinite meaning. At moments we are dissolved with love: "Lord, it is good for us to be here." And with time, sporadic experiences become more abiding realities. Above all, we come to know that the Father is Father, and he is love.

Some time ago I had the privilege of baptizing the newest member of the Pennington clan, little April, born in May. To say she is a beautiful child is a pathetic understatement. As the family gathered for the occasion, I felt the immense amount of love that was being lavished gratuitously upon this newest member. No one seemed to be able to love her enough. And for no other reason than simply because she is. So is the gratuitous love of our Father for us. It is not something that has to be earned. It just is. In fact, it is something more than the sort of gratuitous love we poured out on April. We loved what is this most beautiful little child of God. God's love not only loves what is; God loves what is not, so that it comes to be. God is ever the prodigal Father who rushes out to the sinner—or rather shows up in the sinner's life, for God is always there—as soon as God is given a chance, and changes the bedraggled sinner into the feted child.

It is in the eyes of this love that we come to know ourselves truly. We can really see ourselves only when we see ourselves reflected in the eyes of someone who loves us. But no one can adequately love us, image of God that we are, except God himself. It is when we come to experience ourselves in God's love, in this experience of God at the Center, that we finally come to appreciate our own magnificence, our own true beauty. How this transforms our lives!

When we come to experience how truly magnificent we are, how we are at every moment affirmed by the ever-present creative love of God, we come into a new freedom. No longer do we have to care about what others think of us. No longer need we depend, for a sense of our own worth, on what we accomplish or what we have. We know who we are, and out of that reality we can simply be. And knowing the reality of the infinite creative energy of God in us, we know that we can do all we ever want. "Ask and you shall receive. Seek and you shall have."

Of course, all this does not happen the first time we Center—at least not usually. God is the master of his gifts, and some of us have had transforming experiences of great power right from the start. For most of us, the letting go of the old consciousness to allow the new consciousness to emerge is a gradual process.

When we were baptized and made partakers of the divine
life and nature, we were endowed with certain dispositions
which have traditionally been called the gifts of Holy Spirit.
These potentialities dispose our inner being so that we can
operate under the impulse of Holy Spirit in conformity with
our divinized being. But God profoundly respects our freedom. As long as we insist on functioning on a purely human
level with our natural reasoning and intellectual concepts, God
will not barge in. Our gifts will be dormant. It is only when we
are willing to abandon our very limited human modes of
thought and concepts and open a welcoming space that the
Spirit will begin to operate in us at this divine level. Then we
can begin to experience God as God is in Godself and know
ourselves as we are in God, and know how to act according to
our true divinized nature. When we Center we practice leaving
our human thoughts and reason behind and attending to the
Divine, to the Spirit. Practice moves us toward the perfect. If
we are faithful to our practice, this openness to the Divine will
begin to pervade our lives and we will begin to function out of
this divine sense even when we rise from the Prayer and go
about our daily activity. We will sense the loving, creative presence of God in ourselves and in others and in all things with an
unceasing constancy.

This is the way we come to that constant prayer that our
Lord commanded of us. It is a fruit of Centering Prayer. A
grandmother wrote recently of this kind of prayer:

> When you wake up in the morning and find yourself
> in the presence again, it has an effect on how you act,
> talk, look at yourself, and so forth. It affects every-
> thing. That doesn't mean that you don't remain hu-
> man and fallible. I'm not heaping praise on myself. I
> am simply saying that if you give it half a chance, the
> mystery, the presence of God, bears in on you, even on
> the likes of me. The presence is there and when we
> begin to see it and pick it up and sense it and connect,
> it seems to me that that is legitimate prayer. That's

"being with." I guess that's a good definition of prayer:
It's being with the one that is present.

Loneliness is one of the great sufferings of our times. Needless to say, such experience of Presence as comes from Centering Prayer has a profound effect on our loneliness. It changes
it into solitude—apartness for Presence. Loneliness is an absence, an emptiness. Solitude is loneliness transformed into a
space within which God, self, and others can show up. This
does not mean we will not still feel loneliness. The Presence
may well, at times, overflow into our feelings and senses, and
then loneliness even at that level will vanish. But more often, it
will remain. We still need our friends and loved ones. But even
with them there will be moments of loneliness. Friends cannot
always be there and their absence makes loneliness all the more
felt. Even the most exquisite experiences of loving presence
create their own experience of loneliness. When we have gone
as far as is humanly possible in loving communion, we know
our heart yet yearns for something more complete, the attainment of which seems impossible this side of the heavenly communion. But knowing the experience of God that can turn up
in solitude we can wisely sublimate our loneliness into that
love which is desire and open yet further space for the inva-
sion of the Divine.

The decision, then, to make Centering Prayer a part of our
lives, to move toward a Centered Life, is a decision to move
from loneliness to solitude. In general, the decision to Center
regularly is a decision to choose a life of quality, to choose
consistently what is truly to our good and to our true happiness. There is nothing in our lives that the experience of God,
which we open to in Centering Prayer, does not transform.

Saint Paul, writing to the Galatians, summed it up this
way: "The fruits of the Spirit are love, joy, peace, patience,
kindness, goodness, trustfulness, gentleness, and chastity."

How can we not love when we begin to perceive persons
and things as they truly are in God, with their tremendous
beauty, a reflection and sharing of his own beauty? As we be-

come more and more one with God, our love becomes more like his, that love that is beyond love—mercy which reaches out in compassion and loves what is not beautiful in order to make it beautiful. A Centered life is a life filled with love.

And it is, therefore, a very joyful life. How can we not be filled with joy if we know that at every moment we have the affirming love of God? How can we not be filled with joy as we perceive the essential beauty of all who surround us and of all that surrounds us?

This does not mean we have become blind or insensitive to the gashes that sin has created in human lives and on the face of the earth. If anything, we are more than ever sensitive to them. We are blessed with a more profound compassion. Yet there is a paradox that is experienced here, one that finds its exemplar at the very heart of the Christian mystery. Our experience is that even as we are keenly alive and enter deeply into that suffering of others, there prevails in our deepest being a profound joy in the reality of the Divine Presence and Love—and some sense that with that Love we can bring ultimate healing. Thus it must have been with Christ on the cross. As he hung there he summed up in his humanity the ultimate of human pain and suffering. He not only experienced the most acute forms of physical suffering in the most sensitive of bodies, but he hung before the God he so loved with the mark of every sin upon him. And yet the One who hung there in such degradation was the blessed God, Son in communion with the Father in the Love who is the Spirit, very Beatitude. Logical little human minds can't put it all together. But the one who Centers comes to experience something of it in his daily life.

Every pain is bedded in the joy that comes from the presence of omnipotent Love. And thus there is peace. That peace that comes when we know that God does indeed have everything under control. Whenever I find my soul agitated or troubled with cares and concern, I know if I look more deeply I will find the agitation flows from a lack of trust. I don't effectively believe that my Father has the power and the love to make a reality those words of Saint Paul: "For those who love

God all things work together unto good." When I am alive to the presence and love of God through Centering, I have no fear about this. And I am in peace. God does have everything under control—all the time and everywhere.

But God works at the divine pace—in time. In eternity, in the eternal "now," God is already enjoying the finished product. The first time I realized that God was placidly enjoying "Saint Basil" while I was still struggling along here in time, I was quite unhappy with the Lord, to say the least. But then the Lord reminded me of Matt Talbot, who lay eighteen years drunk in the gutter before he got up on his feet and became a saint. It hasn't been that bad—yet. God is the master of the divine largess. And all is gift. And if I love God I will wholly respect God and want God to be free to act and to accomplish in the way God wants. Yes, for those who love God all things work together unto good, even the way God goes about doing things. I will be patient. With God—and with others. For is it not God who is acting in and through them? If they are failing, it is only because they have not yet received or accepted certain virtues or insights. This is all in God's providence. I have only to look back at my own life. In spite of all the good will I had, how often I have failed—and still do fail—because I do not see or understand. Our Lord's words are so right: "Father, forgive them for they do not know what they do." I have never met a truly malicious person—one who freely chooses evil as evil. We choose the good. But in our blindness or shortsightedness we often choose the partial good, the less good, or the evil masquerading as good. Having learned to accept my own sin, I can accept the sin of others.

Denying sin, denying guilt, does not do any good. Even as our ignorance pardons much of our guilt, our guilt lies in our ignorance—in our "closedness" to the truth and the light. I don't want to lay a guilt trip on anyone. But it doesn't help us to deny true guilt when it is there. The denial will not fool any one. Deep down we know our guilt and need to acknowledge it. But even as we acknowledge it, we know we have a Savior in our Lord Jesus. He has already made up for all our guilt and is in the process of healing in us all the effects of our sin. We can find true joy in this: that we have so good a Savior, such a God of Love, and that our Lord Jesus is glorified in being our compassionate Savior.

We can reason to all this, as I seem to be doing here. But if it were solely a thing of reason, it would not flow into our everyday life with consistency. When we know it through Centering Prayer, it is an effective experience. The Spirit is present and actively creating it in our lives.

When all of this rings true to us, when it is known and known experientially, then we are kind persons, we are gentle persons, and we are good persons. Identifying more and more with God in the divine creative goodness, knowing more and more clearly our oneness with everyone in God's creative love, we want only to do that which will assist others in their goodness and make life good for them. This can profoundly change the activity of our lives. Realizing how everything at every moment flows from the creative goodness of God, we understand how God has willed that our prayer should in some way determine how God will bring forth this creation today, tomorrow, and the next day. With this consciousness we may well be moved to spend more time in prayer, more constantly bring our concerns to the Lord.

We will find ourselves making more room to help others. A young woman writes:

> During the past year since learning Centering Prayer Holy Spirit has led me to two additional ministries (I have already been involved with high school CCD for seven years). I now volunteer three hours a week at our shelter for battered women as a counselor assistant. It has been a most exhilarating experience because I know I can give them Jesus. I can love these women I have never seen before. Then Sunday afternoons I visit an elderly lady in a nursing home who is ignored by her relatives. She'd probably rather have them visit, but she has to be satisfied with me!

Having experienced the difference that the Prayer can make in their lives, most who practice Centering Prayer soon find themselves sharing it with others. This sometimes develops into an apostolate that demands a good bit of time and loving care. I spoke of Dan above. Vin is another example. A recovering alcoholic, he has gone so far as to set up a corporate entity to offer workshops on Centering Prayer not only to his fellow alcoholics but also to true seekers who have been alienated from institutional religions.

Even greater sacrifices may be called forth from us. I have already mentioned the woman who after only a few months of Centering realized the need to leave a high-paying job in a laboratory which was contributing to the creation of nuclear armaments. She knew she had to have a job that was "life-giving." That is goodness.

When we are Centered and in touch with reality, we are trustful persons. We can trust God because we know God's great love and care. We can trust others because we know God's powerful love works in and through them, and everything works together unto good. We can trust the fallible because we know the Infallible stands behind them, writing straight with crooked lines. We can trust that ultimately the will of God will be accomplished in all things. God's kingdom will come. And it is for this that we all pray.

Chastity flows from reverence—reverence in the face of the beauty of our own bodies and every other body as it comes forth every moment as the gift of Creative Love. These bodies may not be used or abused, but only reverently enjoyed in ways that respect their true wonder. This does not mean that we do not still know the impulses of a vigorous sexuality. But when this cannot be expressed in a way that is worthy of the body and of the spirit that is one with it and of the Spirit who dwells within it, we can sublimate this energy. Just as we sublimate the force of loneliness into a desire that is a true love that opens yet more space for the Divine in our lives. This all sounds quite theoretical until it is known and supported by the kind of experience that comes from Centering Prayer.

Besides these benefits which enrich, enliven, and elevate human life, there are many other rewards which contribute to a fuller, happier life. Some of them may seem to be quite natural effects, concomitants of the Prayer. But they are less apt to prove illusory in the context of the essential and complete fulfillment the Prayer brings into our lives.

Dr. Herbert Benson published a very interesting book. The Harvard professor had worked years ago with Maharishi Mahesh Yogi, testing the effects of transcendental meditation on the physical system of the meditator. After a time he broke with the Maharishi and produced a book, *The Relaxation Response*, in which he suggested that meditators use the simple word "one." He found that those who did received as much benefit from their meditation as did meditators who used the Maharishi's assigned mantras. More recently Dr. Benson published a volume called *After the Relaxation Response*, reporting a finding that was for him, a professed agnostic, quite surprising. He discovered two different effects among those who had been taught his relaxation technique.

In the case of some, after an initial period during which the practitioner experienced some good effects in the lessening of tension, a new tension began to mount. The openness that was achieved led to a new experience of emptiness and meaninglessness. Others, however, quite unexpectedly began to thank the doctor for helping them refind God and a meaningful relation with him in prayer. In the space opened by the practice, God had turned up and an earlier faith was revived. The natural benefits found a fulfilling context within which to flourish.

Centering Prayer will release tension. The experience of God's loving and affirming presence, as we have already seen, creates an inner peace. In addition, there is a natural process at work. Just as the flow of dreams in sleep releases the tensions we have built up in the waking state, so the flow of thoughts and images, which takes place while we rest deeply in God, carries away tensions and refreshes the psyche. The thoughts that most strongly attempt to pull us out of the Prayer are those that have the strongest hold on us and are causing the most tension. If we return to them we will but build up more tension around them. But if we let them go and let them flow while we return gently to the Center, they will flow away with their concomitant tension. If we must return to them later, we will find them less burdened and less burdensome.

The deep rest the body receives as the spirit rests in God in the Center enables it to let go of tensions stored in its muscles, organs, and skin. Sometimes we will even dramatically experience this with a jerk or a twist as some knot of tension breaks loose. More often we just experience a greater sense of tranquillity, ease, and peace.

Because we do get a profound rest during the Prayer and tensions are released, one of the things many discover is that they need less sleep when they meditate regularly. Many of us have psychologically set ourselves to need a certain amount of sleep. With our new sense of self and freedom and of being in touch with the Creative Source within us, we can let go of that conditioning and discern our true needs. More than a few, who feared at first that they could not afford the forty minutes a day for Centering Prayer, found after a while that they had actually gained time because of the reduction of time spent in sleep.

The effects of Centering Prayer gain us time in many other ways. The relaxed openness and receptivity to God and his creation enables us to absorb things more quickly and more completely. Our memory is more retentive and available to us. Students and researchers especially appreciate this.

Persons in counseling, personnel, and sales have appreciated how their increased openness and true benignity create a climate in which the client more immediately feels accepted and understood. The rapport is excellent and much of the defensive posturing is left aside. A good bit of time is gained. The worker can readily sense that the manager is concerned about his or her well-being. The customer can experience that the salesperson is coming out of the space of wanting to make a contribution to the customer's life.

Centering by groups at the beginning of a meeting has the

same effect intensified. Centering together, the participants experience their deep unity and emerge from the Prayer with a sense of being together in what they want to accomplish. They are more ready to accept one another's input as a positive contribution.

Of those who have Centered regularly, many have witnessed a heightening of their own creativity. I have personally experienced this in the area of writing. Artists have attested to the same. Also businessmen—especially the entrepreneurial types. A creative mind in business keeps one ahead, at the cutting edge.

I have already spoken of joy, but I want to speak of it again—because all of these things lead to a greater joy in life: less tension, greater effectiveness, greater response, greater productivity, and greater creativity. The glory of God is a person fully alive. The joy of a person is to be that glory, to be fully alive.

There is a challenge here.

If we go to Centering Prayer seeking any of these benefits, we will not get them. For we will not really be in the Prayer; we will still in some way be seeking self instead of seeking God. This is the essence of the Prayer: it is seeking God. It is in some way dying to self, leaving self behind to reach out totally to God. It is the first great commandment lived: love the Lord your God with your whole mind, your whole heart, your whole soul, and your whole strength. There is no room for self in that. The whole is to God in love. This obviously calls for purity of heart, something not come by in a day, ordinarily. But God remains the prodigal Father. If we humbly do what we can and start the journey, God will quickly reach out to our weakness and bring it to completion.

When we pray as purely as we can, we do get all these benefits, and more besides: "Eye has not seen, nor ear heard, nor has it entered into the human heart what God has prepared for those who love God ." The sum of the fruits of Centering Prayer is untold, even by God.

If we do go to the Prayer still clinging to self, more concerned about the benefits of God than the God of benefits, we will not lose all. Some of the natural benefits will still flow through, as they do in any good, natural meditation practice. But these are very little compared to what prayer, contemplative prayer, Centering Prayer in its fullness can bring: endless growth in joy, fulfillment, love, and life.

Refining the Rules

Centering Prayer is a very ancient Christian method or way of prayer, more ancient indeed than the rosary or the Stations of the Cross or almost any other common Christian practice. Monks and nuns, lay folks and clerics, have used this way of prayer through fifteen, sixteen, seventeen, eighteen centuries. This is not surprising, for it is in a way so "natural" and so effective.

What is new about Centering Prayer is the formulation—and the name. In times past, spiritual fathers and mothers would have taught this way of prayer to their disciples in a few words, guiding and refining the disciple's understanding of it in subsequent meetings. The relatively few fathers and mothers who have written of the Prayer have spoken of it in the context of their more general teaching on the whole of the spiritual path. No effort was made to make a precise presentation of the method in itself. Abba Isaac, as reported by Saint John Cassian, came the closest to this.

This has been the challenge of our times. Spiritual fathers and mothers are few and far between; seekers are multitudinous. The tradition has been virtually lost to the community at large. Masters from other traditions are offering their methods in simple, practical ways. The time came to formulate this effective and practical method from our tradition in some simple way so that it could be easily handed on.

Such formulation is not an easy task. Conciseness rules out nuance. The simple formula can be easily misunderstood. This is the great advantage of learning Centering Prayer at a workshop or retreat where the learner can practice the Prayer repeatedly and have ample opportunity to ask questions and share with others. But such an opportunity is not available to everyone. Many, in all parts of the world, have learned the Prayer from books, articles, and tapes. Hence the value of a book such as this, where most of what is said is not new but is expressed in a different way. This new expression will, perhaps, provide that added insight for which the reader has been looking and by which he or she will be encouraged.

Any reader who has followed my writings through the years since we first formulated the three "rules" will have noted an evolution in the way the "rules" are presented. Perhaps we can look at that, and it will show how our understanding has been refined.

I have put "rules" in quotes because I have always been uncomfortable with that word. I can imagine many of the holy fathers rolling over in their graves as I say "rules." Rules for prayer? Rules for making love, for being to one's Friend and Beloved? But what should we call these: points? guidelines? steps? I have not found a satisfactory word. And so we keep on speaking of rules.

It is precisely in this regard that there is an important difference between Christian prayer and methods of meditation passed on by some other traditions. Natural methods depend on the method. And so there are rules spelling out exactly what must be done in order to obtain the desired effect. Christian prayer does not work that way. While it might use a method and be supported by it, Christian prayer depends on Holy Spirit. It always maintains a radical freedom in regard to method. "Where the Spirit is, there is freedom." The Spirit is love. Christian prayer is love; it is a communication in love. It is the encounter between two free persons. No matter what we do, we cannot force the response of the Other. God always remains eminently free in his response.

This is a concern some have had about using a method. Are we trying to force God to give us contemplation? No. But since he respects our freedom, we are using our freedom to open the space so that he can give us the gift of himself in contemplative prayer. In a sense, it might be said we are applying some "pressure" on God. God is faithful. And God has said, "Seek and you shall find." If we seek God, seek an experiential union with the Lord, then God who is faithful will give it to us. However, it is not quite as simple as that. For God knows that in all our seeking we are honestly seeking what is best for us, what God knows is best for us, what God wants. This is present in all our honest seeking. And God responds accordingly. If we seek it, God will infallibly give us the gift of contemplative union with Godself, but God will give it at a time and in a way that is best for us and for our true happiness. We can trust the Lord, God is faithful and true. And infinitely wise. God wants our good and our happiness far more than we do ourselves. I have, in fact, never known anyone who has practiced Centering Prayer faithfully who has not found far more than he or she initially sought. And we seek ever more so that we may receive ever more.

Our initial formulation of the "three rules" was published in *Daily We Touch Him* in 1977. This formulation was repeated almost verbatim in *Centering Prayer* in 1980, but with a number of questions and reservations. A new formulation was not attempted at that time. Perhaps it is now time to reformulate the "rules." Let us look at the original formulation and see where the problems lie.

THE THREE RULES

Rule One:

> At the beginning of the Prayer we take a minute or two to quiet down and then move in faith to God dwelling in our depths; and at the end of the Prayer we take several minutes to come out, mentally praying the Our Father.

Rule Two:

> After resting for a bit in the Center in faith-full love, we take up a single, simple word that expresses the response and begin to let it repeat itself within.

Rule Three:

> Whenever in the course of the Prayer we become aware of anything else, we simply, gently return to the prayer word.

In the course of hundreds of workshops and retreats with thousands of people, responding to tens of thousands of questions, the problem areas of this formulation have become more and more apparent.

The greatest problem has always been that of simplicity. I believe our Lord was pointing toward simplicity when he said, "Unless you become as a little child you will not enter the Kingdom." Simplicity is certainly necessary if we are going to enter into that Kingdom which is within at the Center of our being. But we find simplicity so difficult. We want to make things complicated so that we have more excuse to pay attention to ourselves: See how we are struggling with this! What a mastermind am I to work this one out! Etc.

Last spring I was invited to share Centering Prayer at a center for alcoholic priests. As I was leaving I was presented with a big picture, handsomely framed. (You should have seen me walking through New York with it!) It now hangs over my desk. It shows two seals rubbing noses under the caption: K.I.S.S. Anyone familiar with AA will know what that means (depending on the day): "Keep It Simple, Sweety" or "Keep It Simple, Stupid." (It usually means the latter for me.) I think I will make that the motto of the Centering Prayer Movement: K.I.S.S. Each time you center, KISS yourself.

This is why we have found the beginning of our formulation problematic: "At the beginning of the Prayer we take a minute or two to quiet down...."

First of all, this is not a part of the Prayer as such, but a prelude to it. But what people, in teaching the Prayer, have done with it! That quieting down has turned into some stretching exercises, some yoga, some Silva Mind Control, some hypnotic countdown, some breathing techniques, etc., etc. One teacher ended up urging an hour's prayer rather than two shorter periods because it took so long to get through the quieting-down routine he had developed and had imposed on those whom he taught.

Quite naturally, we will quiet down when we sit to pray. Some of us who tend to rush into things might need a bit of a reminder to take that moment that it takes to settle and relax. Sometimes we will need to do a little something to get rid of some of the body tension. That is why at workshops we do offer some exercises or relaxation techniques. *But they are not part of Centering Prayer.*

Nor should they be taught as part of the Prayer. Nor as a necessary preamble. Each will find what works for him or her. All can be encouraged to do this. Suggestions can be given. But don't let us burden ourselves or others with a long, complex liturgy of "quieting down." The author of *The Cloud of Unknowing*, wise old father that he was, says all that needs to be said: "Simply sit relaxed and quiet."

The author says, "Sit." The question comes up often enough, "Can I walk while I Center?"

Certainly it is possible to bring walking into Centering. At advanced or intensive Centering Prayer workshops we do introduce walking practice or meditation. The purpose is to take the first steps toward bringing Centering into our whole life, or bringing our whole life into the Center. In a word: integration. But we will always want those periods when we are wholly Centered. In the beginning, until we are living a fully Centered life, we will need them. While we walk, at least some little part of our attention must necessarily attend to the operation of placing one foot before the other. We are not free to attend wholly and simply to God. When we sit in repose, eyes gently closed, we can.

At this point my conclusion is that it might be best not to say anything about the preliminaries in the three guidelines themselves.

The next problem comes up with the word "move." What do we mean here by "move"? What kind of movement is it? The author of *The Cloud* tells us: "Center all your attention and desire on him." The movement here is precisely Centering. We focus our mind's attention and our heart's desire on the Lord present at the Center of our being.

This statement of the author points to one of the serious lacunae in our formulation, which speaks only of faith and says nothing of our desire. While it does speak of "faith-filled love" in the second rule, the omission of love here is a real mistake. It is not enough to know, even in faith, that God is present in the Center of our being. Even the devils know and acknowledge that. Such knowledge is not prayer. It is the response to that presence with the gift of ourselves in love that makes this prayer. So we must move in faith and love.

I am still not sure that "move" is the right word here. It seems to imply more activity than is really called for. In an appendix in *Centering Payer* I offered a few examples of the movement in faith and love. Perhaps that was a mistake. Looking at them now I find them too long and complicated. In practice, I find that people, especially when they are leading the Centering Prayer in a group, tend to formulate long and beautiful prayers that surely invite us to get caught up in concepts and images instead of simply being to God in love. I think that this might be the better word: "Be." Be in faith and love to God present at the center of our being.

I like the word "dwelling," though, for it is more biblical. The Lord promised at the supper on the night before he died that he and the Father will dwell in us if we love him, truly love him by keeping his commandments. This dwelling is something more than God's ontological presence in all creatures. God dwells in us as one who shares a home, as a friend, a lover.

So let us be in faith and love to God who dwells in the center of our being.

What does this mean? It means we let everything else go and turn our full attention on the Lord whom we know by faith to be present in us. He said he would take up his dwelling in us and we know he is true to his word. So we acknowledge his presence there, even though we may not sense it; even though our reason may not be able to prove it—indeed, may challenge the reality of it. We know he is there, our Father who loves us, our Friend who makes up for all our lacks and failures and shortcomings. We respond to that love as best we can by giving ourselves. We give God our time, our attention, our love, and our very selves, as completely as we can for these few minutes. We choose God as the Center of our lives, the Center beyond our self center. We are ready to let God be our Lord, our Master and Teacher, the one who decides how we live. That is the whole Prayer. We give our selves to God as completely as we can. We let the Lord have us and hold us and love us as he will. It is that simple, that total.

Rule One goes on to speak of what happens at the end of the Prayer. As I suggested in Centering Payer, I think, however consecrated the number three is, it might be better to place this at the end, rather than combining it with the first guide.

So, for now, let us move on to *Rule Two*.

Again, my experience calls for simplicity. There is no need to say, "After residing for a bit...." That just happens. To speak of it only invites self-reflection and complexity. People begin to worry about the "bit."

The expression "a single, simple word that expresses the response" is inspired by *The Cloud*. Again, I think it could be said more simply. Just take up a love word. That is the response we are talking about—love. Such a word is bound to be a simple word. And it will almost always be a single word. If it isn't, no matter, so long as it is indeed a love word.

People worry about this word. Much too much is made of it. Perhaps this is due to seepage from other traditions. In some Hindu traditions where mantric meditation is practiced, the mantra is always given by the master. When Transcendental Meditation came to this country, much was made of transmission of the mantra. The mantra itself was cloaked with a certain secret power. The prayer word is nothing like that. It is a powerful word. It has all the power of our love. It is the word that spontaneously expresses our love. In most cases it will be the name of the Beloved: Lord, God, Father, Jesus. Or it may be, as the author of *The Cloud* suggests, simply the word "love." It matters little what it is. Just let it be a simple word that expresses our being to our God in love.

The rest of *Rule Two* also invites confusion because of the assimilation of ideas from mantric meditation—an important form of meditation among Hindus. Mantric meditation involves repeating a particular word, sound, or formula constantly until the sound brings one into an altered state of consciousness. It is, of course, possible to inform such a practice with faith and love and turn it into a Christian form of meditation. This is what Father John Main has done. We will speak of this in the next chapter. But our use of the prayer word, the word of love, is not mantric. Our mode of transcendence, of going beyond our ordinary consciousness, of going beyond ourselves, is not through the effects of sound. Our going beyond ourselves is an outreach of love to the Infinite. As Saint Thomas Aquinas says, "Where the mind leaves off, love goes on."

The use of the love word in Centering Prayer is to support us in abiding in the state of being to the Lord in love. While we abide with the Lord we do not consciously use the word. It is there in the mind, our chosen word, ready to be used whenever we need it, according to the *Third Rule*: to return or simply to reinforce our being to the Lord in love. Some days we will quite consciously and deliberately take the prayer word up after our initial movement of faith and love. And this might be most often the case until we settle down. But there will be times when we come to the Lord and need little help simply to be with him in love.

We don't have to aim at repeating the word. Being there, it will tend to repeat itself. All our attention is on the Lord (as the author of *The Cloud* said, "Center all your attention and desire on him"), not on the word. Nor on the practice, on ourselves, or on anything else—only on the Lord.

There are two kinds of love or experiences of love: love of desire and love of delight. Love of delight is the pleasure we experience when we are in the presence of someone or something we love. Love of desire is that love which reaches out for the beloved when we experience his or her absence. The author of *The Cloud* speaks of desire, since the experience of God when one enters into the cloud of unknowing is as if God were in fact absent. This is the more common experience in Centering, at least at the beginning. God is truly with us, of course, never absent. It is God's presence and grace that draws us, otherwise we would not seek him. But we sense only the darkness and in that darkness our love reaches out to God in desire. "My soul longs for the Lord." It is in such darkness, in such longing, that we may well need the support of our word of love. When God is experienced as present, we hardly need a word to assist us in remaining present to God. Our whole being is drawn into the enjoyment of God's love, of God's very Self. Our self is to God's Self in a unity that is beyond our imaging or expressing.

So we take up this love word and let it be gently present, supporting our being to God in faith-filled love.

Already in Centering Prayer, I began some reformulation of *Rule Three*: "Whenever in the course of the Prayer we become aware of anything else, we simply gently return to the Presence by the use of the prayer word."

The original formulation was poor. It tended to lead prayers to make too much of the word—to attend to the word instead of to the Lord. The revised formula seems adequate.

The emphasis remains on the word "aware." What we are concerned about here is that state in which we tend to be so much of the time—one step removed from reality, watching ourselves do what we do, experience what we experience, instead of being wholly in the experience. So long as we are with the Lord, it little matters what goes on. It is entirely up to God. The child is in the arms of her Father and the Father is content. It is when we come back to self and are aware of ourselves, aware of what we are doing, that we are no longer simple. We are divided. We are doing what we are doing and, at the same time, we are watching ourselves do it. As long as we are fully in what we are doing, we are not aware of what we are doing. This is why the word "else" in our formulation could be deceptive. Even awareness that we are praying to God divides us and detracts from our being wholly to God. As the Fathers say: "So long as one is aware one is praying, one is not yet praying." As the author of *The Cloud* says, "Center all [not just part of] your attention...on God...." In this sense, too, the Prayer is utterly simple. There is no division.

When we are introducing the Prayer we recommend at least two 20-minute periods of Centering Prayer a day. It is good that this be accepted as a given, for the beginner does not yet have the means to discern otherwise. When our lives become fully Centered, we will be able to discern how much pure Centering we need to remain fully and peacefully in this state of consciousness. We will always want a certain amount of Centering Prayer just to enjoy the Lord and let the Lord enjoy us.

The second part of *Rule One* might well be placed after the third guide. This might make the movement of the Prayer clearer.

This point, too, might be expressed more simply. We just want the Lord's Prayer, or whatever other prayer we decide upon, to emerge out of the deep silence, to bring our experience up to the conceptual and affective level, insofar as this is possible. For this reason it is well if we choose one prayer and use it habitually, so that the formula, the words, will demand the least amount of attention and the experience can emerge. During this concluding prayer, as thoughts gather around the words and call forth affections, we do attend to them. It is time for God whom we have experienced at the Center to teach us, to expand our consciousness even at the conceptual level, to inflame and soften our hearts with all the movements of love. Especially compassion, the being with the other—God and all those in God, everyone in all the movements of their hearts.

I do not think we have to worry about the time frame here. If we allow each phrase to open out, the Prayer will take long enough. Again, it is a question of being more to what is, and what is happening, than of following a method or doing it right.

Because this is such a different movement of prayer, perhaps it is best not to consider it as a fourth guide, but rather let it be an appendix (just as the settling down or posturing is a prelude) and stay with

THREE RULES OR GUIDES

Sit relaxed and quiet.

1. Be in faith and love to God who dwells in the center of your being.
2. Take up a love word and let it be gently present, supporting your being to God in faith-filled love.
3. Whenever you become aware of anything, simply, gently return to the Lord with the use of your prayer word.

Let the Our Father (or some other prayer) pray itself.

Remember always that Centering Prayer is, first of all and above all, an interpersonal relationship—a very privileged one, for the other Person is God. It is a communion and union in love. In relation to this, everything else is secondary and consequential.

Contemplation and Method

When we first began to teach Centering Prayer in our retreat house we called it simply "contemplative prayer." This created problems for some, especially priests and religious. One priest told me about his course in ascetical and mystical theology. After they had studied all about acquiring the virtues and the different forms of active and discursive prayer, they arrived at the section on contemplative prayer. The priest-professor closed the book: "That will be of no interest to you. Unless perhaps you are made chaplain to some Carmelites, then you can bone up on it." The implication, of course, was that contemplative prayer was not for busy, active priests. Religious were often given the impression in the course of their novitiate training that if they were very faithful to discursive meditation day in and day out then someday, perhaps, after years and years, contemplation would drop out of heaven upon them. But to seek it beforehand would be presumption and pride, delusion and self-seeking. This being the experience of priests and religious, you can imagine the response of lay persons. Or can you? Actually they were, for the most part, more open to the idea of all being called to contemplative prayer.

Priests who had kept the book open and studied further about the Christian life were very quickly asking us whether Centering Prayer leads to acquired or infused contemplation. Authors are by no means in agreement on how to define these two states or stages of prayer—acquired and infused contemplation—and on how to distinguish between them. In general, acquired contemplation can be considered to be that prayer which flows from human activity, using to the full the infused graces of faith, hope, and charity. Infused contemplation, on the other hand, can be seen rather as being God's work, bringing into activity the gifts of Holy Spirit.

When we are baptized and come into grace we receive certain dispositions or powers of soul, of mind and heart, whereby we can hear God's revealed word and accept it and respond in love. These dispositions are called the infused virtues of faith, hope, and charity. Their operation in us is still very much governed by the human mind albeit under the movement of God's grace and at a level that is above what is naturally possible. At the moment of our christening, we also receive some other dispositions, which we call the gifts. These open the way for Holy Spirit to operate in our minds and hearts, enabling us to function according to the divine way of acting. Under the operation of the gifts we do not reason to things, nor know them just by hearing. In some way we actually know them by experience. We sense God and the things of God somewhat as God does. God is operative in us, immediately revealing Godself present to us. "Taste and see how good the Lord is." Taste is a good image. The experience is within, immediate, and certain.

We receive these dispositions for the Spirit to act in us when we come into Christ. But in many people's lives they are for the most part left to lie dormant. God is infinitely patient. God will not push into our lives. God knows the greatest thing given us is our freedom, for therein lies our power to love. God respects our freedom. If we want habitually, even exclusively, to operate at the level of our own reason, God will respectfully keep silent. We can fill ourselves with our own thoughts, ideas, images, and feelings. God will not interfere. But if we invite God with attention, opening the inner space with silence, God will begin to speak to our souls, not in words or concepts but in the mysterious way that love expresses itself—by presence.

The point at which a prayer ceases to be acquired and becomes infused is not easy to discern, even if one has clearly distinguished between them. God is certainly present and active in all prayer, otherwise we would not pray. All prayer is a response to the call of God's love with the love God has given to us.

Is it important to know whether our prayer is acquired or infused contemplation? In practice, I do not think so. Certainly, if at the time we are supposed to be praying we are examining whether our prayer is acquired or infused, we are, in fact, not praying. We are wrapped up in ourselves as a specimen.

It might be important for those of us much attached to discursive meditation, running our prayer as we run our life, to realize that it is time to let go a bit—let go and let God: let God have a little room to work in us through Holy Spirit. We all know that no relationship works if one of the parties is trying to be totally in control.

Here we see the immense benefit of Centering Prayer. At least for these twenty minutes, we can let go and let God. The method is so absolutely simple that in the space opened God can draw us to Godself in whatever way God wishes. Our Centering Prayer may be a deep, quiet, affective prayer. Or, it may be the time when God enlivens in us the convictions of faith and directs us to action. We are most receptive to this during the Prayer, for both eyes are fully on God. It may be a time of simple contemplation, when we rest in God's presence and love, directing our attention to God by gentle acts of the will expressed in the prayer word of love. Or, God may do all the drawing, and we taste and see. For our part, the Prayer is always pure gift. We give ourselves in love and then leave the rest to God.

Centering Prayer certainly tends toward infused contemplation. It is a powerful statement to God that we do want the graces of contemplation, that delightful experience of God's presence and love. It opens the door wide to let God act freely in us, especially through the Spirit's gifts of wisdom and understanding.

"Wisdom" translates the Latin word *sapientia*, from the root *sapor*, savor. Through the activity of the graces of this *gift* we savor God wherever God is to be found. Understanding—to stand under—means to get inside the reality of things. The

Latin word is *intelligere*, from the Latin *inter*, within, and *legere*, to read: to read what is within. The gift of understanding enables us then to see reality from within, seeing in the Center of every person and every thing the Lord in all his creative love, bringing them forth in love, seeing each person in his or her truest being, as the image of God, made in his likeness, radiating, in spite of any overlay of sin, the divine beauty. How easy it is to love when we are experiencing life at this level.

If you have not yet experienced it, try to imagine what life will be like when these gifts become habitually operative in your life. Is it a wonder that people get excited about Centering Prayer when it opens up for them this dimension of life? Is it too much of an exaggeration to speak about "heaven on earth"—for what else is heaven but the fullest experience and enjoyment of God and everyone else in God? It can begin here.

In spite of the fact that contemplation is so wonderful, so simple, so obviously meant to be a part of any prayer life, so much a part of our tradition, it seems that too many fears and prejudices are aroused when one speaks of the Prayer as contemplation or contemplative prayer.

My confrere, Father William, chose to speak of it as the Prayer of *The Cloud*. This is good. It highlights a source of the teaching in our tradition—a source readily available: *The Cloud of Unknowing*—showing that this simple form of prayer is indeed a part of our tradition and not something brought in from outside.

How helpful the image of the cloud is, I am not sure. Thomas Merton, in one of his Sunday-afternoon conferences with the monks at Gethsemani not long before his final journey, rather joshed at it:

> ...you just beat your head against this cloud of unknowing—it gets you up just a little bit above the stratosphere and no higher and you are beating your head against the cloud of unknowing and you are treading everything down under the cloud of forgetting and you are just floating.

It was at the first workshop I held outside the monastery for a group of religious superiors that Father Armand Proux began to use the term "Centering Prayer." And the name caught on.

I think it is a good name. We do need to use some image when we speak of prayer. The "Prayer of the Heart," a more traditional and biblical name for the Prayer, has its problems today. Besides the fact that some are prone to take the image too graphically and start constructing little doors and windows and rooms in their hearts, the pervasive influence of modern medicine in our society tends to conjure up memories of bypasses, artificial hearts, and pacemakers. The biblical image does not easily come through.

On the other hand "center" is an almost imageless image. Try to imagine your center, your very center. You are drawn deeper and deeper, beyond all images, into the ground of your being. From there, as Merton says, we can easily pass through our center into the very Center of God. Merton it was who inspired the name. And Merton it is who is undoubtedly the most articulate, complete, and insightful writer of our times, if not of all times, on this kind of prayer. We will look at his teaching shortly.

At the time we began to use the term "Centering Prayer," it was wholly novel. Indeed, Father William objected to it because of this novelty. He feared it might sound gimmicky. But the name stuck and in time became quite popular. Then many began to use it and use it in many ways. We had not put a copyright on it! This is unfortunate, I think. While method is very secondary and subservient in prayer, it can be very helpful, especially if it is clear and simple. When different teachers speak of "Centering Prayer," each giving it a different meaning, applying the term to different methods, clarity suffers. I would like to try to sort things out a bit.

Teachers do speak of centering in pottery, of centering in song, of centering on some external image. This is not wrong, of course. Centering is a perfectly good English word and can be applied to many things.

There can be many ways of praying that are real "centering" prayers, opening out into contemplation. I think of that beautiful and favorite story of the man who sat long hours in the church of the Curé of Ars. One day the saintly Curé asked the man what he was doing through all those hours. His response—so simple: "I look at him, and he looks at me." He was, indeed, centering—centering on the tabernacle. Many of my manuscripts have been typed by a wonderful little nun, a Benedictine of Perpetual Adoration. When she has finished her daily typing she goes to the church and kneels before the altar, her eyes, her heart, her whole being, centered on the eucharistic Lord enthroned in the monstrance. She is indeed "Centering." After Communion I think we all tend to center on the Lord within us in the Eucharist. Our Byzantine sisters and brothers in their prayer often center upon the real presence in an icon.

These are all very valid forms of centering prayer. But I wonder if it is helpful, just because the term has become popular, to speak of them as "Centering Prayer." I think it will only breed confusion and disturb some who have at last found a simple, clear method they can use and do not want to lose hold of it. Later, when they have a more secure hold on their way, such confusion will not trouble them. But as teachers we do want to be especially caring with those who are God's little ones in the life of Prayer.

Judging by the many letters I receive and the questions that are asked, I believe Father Ernest Larkin initially caused a lot of confusion in this regard through his retreats and his tapes. At that time he called "Centering Prayer" any form of prayer that led to interiority. In particular, he spoke of three kinds.

The first for him was the guided imagery which Saint Teresa of Jesus learned from Osuna's *Third Spiritual Alphabet*. This prayer begins with a concrete image of Jesus, usually some scene from the gospels. One abides with the image and if it leads the pray-er further, even to the Source of Being, that is fine. This is a beautiful form of prayer. It reaches to God through biblical image, through images of the Sacred Humanity, and it is open to the pray-er being carried beyond the images to di-

rect experience of God. But I really do not see the value of co-
opting the name "Centering Prayer" for this prayer, which uses
images and in that sense is quite different from Centering Prayer
as such.

Let me skip to Father Larkin's third form of "Centering
Prayer." This is the Ignatian consciousness examen. I must
confess I find it even more difficult to justify calling this "Centering Prayer." In this prayer, one is very much involved in self,
though certainly also with God. It is truly prayer, but it is so
very different from a simple, selfless centering on God.

It is in Father Larkin's second form of "Centering Prayer"
that we find the most confusion. Father calls this "mantric"
prayer. He asserts that this is what is "usually called Centering
Prayer." Then he goes on to say there are two forms—the one
taught by Father John Main, and the other, which we teach.
Father Main never called his method "Centering Prayer." Father Larkin then says things about this "Centering Prayer"
which are true of Father Main's method but are not true of
Centering Prayer (such as "Centering Prayer is saying your
holy word"). He also says things which are not true of either
method, if I understand Father Main well (such as fitting the
word in with one's breathing—this pertains to certain forms
of yogic meditation). In the midst of all this confusion, Father
Larkin seeks to relate this prayer to the teaching of Saint John
of the Cross and Saint Teresa of Jesus, situating it "just before
the prayer of simple regard."

I deeply regret that Centering Prayer is being propagated,
albeit with much good will, with such confusion and complexity. As the author of *The Cloud* says, "Its value lies in its simplicity."

K.I.S.S.

Since Father Larkin has confused Centering Prayer with
the teaching of Father John Main, it might be well to look at
Father John's method in order to see more clearly the difference between these two methods of contemplative prayer.

Father John Main certainly gives witness to the value of
simplicity, both in the method he teaches and in the style of his

paternal teaching. He is a true spiritual father in the best sense of that term in our Christian tradition. The fact that the Lord has shortened his course is something we can only bow down before as an inscrutable mystery. We can be thankful that Father has left a good and strong disciple to continue his teaching.

Perhaps Father's greatest contribution was the creation of a modern institutional form that is, in our times, an apt vehicle for something most precious in the Benedictine heritage: a monastic presence at the heart of the city. A few monks, a small community, supported by an established monastery, stood at the center of a large confluence of laity with varying degrees of commitment and participation, adapted to the particular lay vocation of each. If today's Benedictines could bring such powerful centers of prayer to all our cities we would quickly experience a renewed Church and society.

At the heart of Father Main's community was the regular practice of a contemplative type of prayer, or meditation, as Father preferred to call it. As a diplomat in the British colonial service in Malaysia, Father Main underwent a profound experience when taught mantric meditation by a swami. Later, when he had returned to England and entered Ealing Abbey, he discovered the simple method of prayer taught by Abba Isaac in Saint John Cassian's *Conferences*. Father put the two together, baptized the mantra, as it were, and found a very effective way of gradually bringing himself to inner silence and true contemplative prayer. This is what he taught others, giving them a New Testament mantra: Maranatha.

Since Father had used, in part, the source from which Centering Prayer flows, it is not surprising that there are similarities between the two forms of prayer. The emphasis on simplicity is key to them both. Both use a "word," but in fact in very different ways: herein lies the greatest difference between the two forms. Rather than telling the disciple to choose a word, one that is meaningful to the individual, as does the author of *The Cloud*, or beginning with a meaningful verse of Scripture out of which the disciple's word can emerge, as does

Abba Isaac, Father assigns a word—one that is not apt to have meaning for most, but one that has good sound quality. He then instructs the disciple to use this word as a yogi would use the mantra given by the swami: "If you want to learn to meditate, you must learn to sit still and to say your word from beginning to end....the rule that is most important of all—say your mantra, say your word. And that is the art of meditation, to learn to say it from the beginning to the end." This emphasis on the word, and especially the insistence on saying it without ceasing, is not present in Centering Prayer. It may well happen, especially for beginners, that they will be using their word almost constantly as they continually find themselves back in reflective awareness. But the whole emphasis in Centering Prayer is on the Presence, on the Lord our God in the Center of our being, known by faith and reached by love. The word in Centering Prayer is a love word, and it is used only when it is needed to support the love. The mode of transcendence, of going out of ourselves into God, is love.

Father Main's instruction does not end with the mantra, however much that might seem to dominate it:

> The day will come when the mantra ceases to sound and we are lost in the eternal silence of God. The rule when this happens is not to try to possess the silence, to use it for one's own satisfaction. The clear rule is that as soon as we consciously realize that we are in this state of profound silence and begin to reflect about it we must gently and quietly return to our mantra.

The advice or direction given here is not unlike our *Third Rule.* And the point Father makes is very good. We can even become aware of our silence, and then it is an obstacle to our being purely and simply to God. It is time to use the word again. The difference in Centering Prayer lies in the fact that we use the word simply to return to the Presence, to return to God at the Center of our being.

Father Main does not use the term "center" very often in

his teaching. Actually, the first quotation which I gave from his conferences comes from a talk entitled "The One Centre." In the course of this talk, though, Father only uses the word "centre" five times. What he says is very central:

> Basically, meditation is a way of coming to your own centre [Father was Irish and habitually used the British spelling], the foundation of your own being, and remaining there—still, silent, attentive....The wonderful thing we discover when we get underway is that there is only one centre, that that centre is everywhere and that meditation is the way of being linked to it in our own centre. Because we are then rooted in ourselves we find our place in the universe and so we find the centre of the universe. We find God.

We can certainly agree on this. As we proceed to the second part of this book, seeking a deeper understanding of Centering Prayer, we will want to return to this basic understanding of the Center.

Before moving on, I want to make it very clear that in drawing a comparison between Father John Main's method and Centering Prayer I do not want in any way to be critical of his teaching. I think it is excellent. The Lord leads each of us in different ways. For some, Father's very simple method will be the way. For others, it will be Centering Prayer. And others still, in the Divine leading, will find for themselves something of a mixture that will work. But, as I said before, there is value in being clear in our teaching. And comparison is one way of attaining greater clarity in regard to both of the things compared.

I do want to affirm again my profound respect for this highly-to-be-revered and deeply lamented spiritual father. I think his disciple, Father Laurence, pays him due honor when he writes:

A teacher, a true master of the spiritual life like Fr. John (who would have smiled at such a solemn title), teaches by gaining the attention of the whole person, not just by addressing the mind with ideas or the feelings with emotions. To be taught like this is itself an experience of the spiritual reality....

Deepening Our
Understanding

I n this second part we want to seek to deepen and broaden our understanding of the full potential of Centering Prayer.

Why do we seek such understanding? It is something quite natural to the human mind to want to understand more fully the things with which it comes into contact. Witness the incessant whys of the child. Faith, too, seeks understanding. This is the very substance of theology.

A fuller understanding, however, is valuable to us for many other reasons than simply satisfying our desire to learn. Such an understanding increases our appreciation of the Reality and its potential in our lives, giving us a greater willingness to open ourselves and to do what we need to do for the realization of this potential. It safeguards us from being deflected in our progress by alluring substitutes, simulations, or pleasant asides with clear knowledge we are not apt to mistake the accidental elements for the substance of the Reality. Rather, we see more and more clearly how the Reality—and it alone—can fulfill all our deepest aspirations.

Perhaps no one in our times has written with more understanding about this kind of prayer than Thomas Merton (Father Louis of Gethsemani). I invite you to reflect with me on a number of the more relevant passages of his writings. Then we will develop more fully some of the theology underlying Centering Prayer.

Thomas Merton and Centering Prayer

Thomas Merton, in his book *The Contemplative Life*, spoke about centering prayer and would say things like this:

> The fact is, however, that if you descend into the depths of your own spirit...and arrive somewhere near the center of what you are, you are confronted with the inescapable truth, at the very root of your existence, you are in constant and immediate and inescapable contact with the infinite power of God.

And like this:

> *A man cannot enter into the deepest center of himself and pass through the center into God unless he is able to pass entirely out of himself and empty himself and give himself to other people in the purity of selfless love* (New Seeds of Contemplation—Merton's italics).

In my first book on Centering Prayer, I offered a number of texts from the writings of Merton on this kind of prayer. But nowhere in the writings he published have we found a really personal expression of his own use of the Prayer. Merton was a very private person. Although he published an autobiography and a number of personal journals, these were all carefully edited. However, in his letters Merton was sometimes quite open, especially with spiritual persons whom he felt were aligned with him, even though they were of very different traditions. It is in a letter to a Sufi scholar, Aziz Ch. Abdul, that Merton gives a rather long and clear description of his ordinary way of praying:

> Now you ask about my method of meditation. Strictly speaking I have a very simple way of prayer. It is centered entirely on attention to the presence of God and to His will and His love. That is to say that it is centered on *faith* by which alone we can know the presence of God. One might say this gives my meditation the character described by the Prophet as "being before God as if you saw Him." Yet it does not mean imagining anything or conceiving a precise image of God, for to my mind this would be a kind of idolatry. On the contrary, it is a matter of adoring Him as invisible and infinitely beyond our comprehension, and realizing Him as all. My prayer tends very much to what you call *fana*. There is in my heart this great thirst to recognize totally the nothingness of all that is not God. My prayer is then a kind of praise rising up out of the center of Nothingness and Silence. If I am still present "myself" this I recognize as an obstacle. If He wills he can then make the Nothingness into a total clarity. If He does not will, then the Nothingness actually seems to itself to be an object and remains an obstacle. Such is my ordinary way of prayer, or meditation. It is not "thinking about" anything, but a direct seeking of the Face of the Invisible. Which cannot be found unless we become lost in Him who is Invisible (*The Hidden Ground of Love*, pp. 63f).

This is quite simply Centering Prayer.

The idea of God as being at the center was brought home to Merton early in his life, in an experiential rather than conceptual way—in a way that spoke to him daily, almost constantly, in one of the most formative periods of his life. When he was ten years old his father took him to live in St. Antonin. This was a medieval shrine town in the Midi that still preserved much of its medieval character when the Mertons moved there in 1925. As a shrine, the church stood prominently at the middle of the town. All streets led to it, or away from it, depending on one's perspective. The impression was unmistakable that the church and the One who dwelt therein were at the center of things. Twenty years later Merton recorded this impression, which daily impinged on the young adolescent:

> ...the center of it all was the church. Here, in this amazing, ancient town, the very pattern of the place, of the houses and streets and of nature itself, the cliffs and trees, all focused my attention upon the one, important central fact of the church and what it contained. Here, everywhere I went, I was forced by the disposition of everything around me, to be always at least virtually conscious of the church. Every street pointed more or less inward to the center of the town, to the church. Every view of the town, from the exterior hills, centered upon the long gray building with its high spire (*The Seven Storey Mountain*, pp. 36f).

In his writings, Merton speaks of the sad effects of not living out of the center, out of the Reality that is:

> We are so obsessed with *doing* that we have no time and no imagination left for *being*. As a result, men are valued not for what they are but for what they *do* or what they *have*—for their usefulness. When man is reduced to his function he is placed in a servile, alienated condition. He exists *for* someone else or even worse for some *thing* else.
>   Those who relinquish God as the center of their moral orbit lose all direction and by that very fact lose and betray their manhood (*Conjectures of a Guilty Bystander*, pp. 282 and 104).

Presupposed to Centering Prayer and the first movement toward it is faith. The journey toward the Center is a journey of faith, nourished by the two sources, Scripture and Tradition—nourished by rich *lectio*, or faith reading and sharing. In a rare instance where Merton shares one of his dreams he speaks to this:

> I dreamt I was lost in a great city and walking "toward the center" without quite knowing where I was going. Suddenly I came to a dead end, but on a height looking at a great bay, an arm of the harbor. I saw a whole section of the city spread out before me on hills covered with light snow, and realized that, though I had far to go, I knew where I was: because in this city there are two arms of the harbor and they help you to find your way, as you are always encountering them (*Conjectures of a Guilty Bystander*, p. 170).

The two arms of the harbor are, of course, Scripture and Tradition. With them there to guide us we cannot get lost on our walk "toward the center." We need to turn to them daily to find our way.

The way to the center, to the experience of God, is love. From love comes our ability to sense God present. Merton goes on to speak of the first movements of this as it might be experienced in Centering Prayer:

> There is a kind of pre-experiential contemplation in which the soul simply plunges into the darkness without knowing why, and tends blindly toward something it knows not. Only later is there a strong, subjective verification of the truth that this "something" toward which the soul is groping is really God Himself and not just an idea of God or a velleity for union with him ("The Inner Experience," *Cistercian Studies* 18:71).

Such a plunging takes courage; it is a thing of grace, but it is only in the experience that we can discover that this is so:

> God is grace to man, grace in such a thorough going sense that it supports the whole of man's existence and can only be conceived of as grace by those who surrender their whole existence and let themselves fall into the unfathomable dizzy depth without seeking for something to hold on to ("A Vow of Conversation," unpublished manuscript).

Merton gives encouraging advice to the beginner:

> Be content, be content. We are the Body of Christ! We have found him because he has sought us. God has come to take up his abode in us, in sinners. There is nothing further to look for except to turn to him completely, where he is already present. Be quiet and see that he is God (*Conjectures of a Guilty Bystander*, p. 14).
>
> If you dare to penetrate your own silence and dare to advance without fear into the solitude of your own heart, and seek the sharing of that solitude with the lonely other who seeks God through and with you, then you will truly receive the light and capacity to understand what is beyond words and beyond explanation because it is too close to be explained: it is the intimate union in the depths of your own heart, of God's spirit and your own secret inmost self, so that you and he are in truth One Spirit (private notes).

A Prayer in Faith

The first "rule" or point in Centering Prayer is to be in faith and love to God dwelling in the depths of our being or at the center of our being.

Merton explains this movement in faith with a clear and important distinction:

If we enter into ourselves, finding our true self, and then passing "beyond" the inner "I," we sail forth into the immense darkness in which we confront the "I am" of the Almighty....Our inmost "I" exists in God and God dwells in it. But it is nevertheless necessary to distinguish the experience of one's own inmost being and the awareness that God has revealed himself to us in and through our inner self. We must know that the mirror is distinct from the image reflected. The difference rests in theological *faith*. Our awareness of our inner self can at least theoretically be the fruit of a purely natural and psychological purification. Our awareness of God is a supernatural participation in the light by which he reveals himself interiorly as dwelling in our inmost self. Hence the Christian mystical experience is not only an awareness of the inner self, but also, by a supernatural intensification of faith, it is an experiential grasp of God as present within our inner self ("The Inner Experience," *Cistercian Studies* 18:9f).

It is faith that tells us most surely that

Christ is really present in us, more present than if he were standing before us visible to our bodily eye....By the gift of the Gospel...we are able to see our inner selves not as a vacuum but as an *infinite depth*, not as emptiness but as fullness. This change of perspective is impossible as long as we are afraid of our own nothingness, as long as we are afraid of fear, afraid of poverty, afraid of boredom—as long as we run away from ourselves....Hence the sacred attitude is one which does not recoil from our own inner emptiness, but rather penetrates into it with awe and reverence and with the awareness of mystery (*ibid*. 18:211ff).

This is the whole of the Prayer, this moving in faith and love to God within. Then we simply abide there, rest there in the Reality:

> In silence, hope, expectation, and unknowing, the man of faith abandons himself to the divine will not as to an arbitrary and magic power whose decrees must be spelt out from cryptic ciphers but as to the stream of reality and of life itself. The sacred attitude is then one of deep and fundamental respect for the real in whatever form it may present itself (*ibid.* 18:215).

There is real abandonment and acceptance of whatever God allows to happen during the time of our Prayer, and yet there is not a deadly passivity. There is a lively presence in faith and hope:

> What happens, happens. One accepts it, in humility, and sees it without inferring anything, or instituting any comparison with other experiences. And one walks on in the presence of God....Would be contemplatives must be on their guard against a kind of heavy, inert stupor in which the mind becomes swallowed up in itself. To remain immersed in one's own darkness is not contemplation, and no one should attempt to "stop" the functioning of his mind and remain fixed in his own nothingness. Rather we must go out in hope and faith from our own nothingness and seek liberation in God (*ibid.* 18:291ff).

It is faith which is at the very heart of this Prayer, it is faith which guides our surrender in love, our mode of transcendence. Merton insists on this again and again:

> ...one must let himself be guided to reality not by visible and tangible things, not by the evidence of sense or the understanding of reason, not by concepts

charged with natural hope, or joy, or fear, or desire, or grief, but by "dark faith" that transcends all desire and seeks no human earthly satisfaction, except what is willed by God and connected with his will (*ibid.* 18:13).

This act of total surrender is not simply a fantastic intellectual and mystical gamble, it is something much more serious: It is an act of love for this unseen Person who in the very gift of love by which we surrender ourselves to his reality also makes himself present to us. The union of our mind, spirit, and life with the Word present within us is effected by Holy Spirit (*ibid.* 18:209).

It is a contact with God in charity, yes, but also and above all in the darkness of unknowing. This follows necessarily from the fact that it goes beyond the symbols and intentions of the intellect, and attains God directly without the medium of any created image. If medium there is, it is not intellectual, not an image or species of the mind, but a disposition of our whole being brought about by that Love which so likens and conforms us to God that we become able to experience him mystically in and through our inmost selves as if he were our very selves. The inner self…now knows God not so much through the medium of an objective image as through its own divinized subjectivity (*ibid.* 18:299).

There seems to be a bit of ambivalence as Merton speaks about this experience. He sees it as something very special indeed. And it does call for a very high level of courage and fidelity. And yet it is meant for all, it is the common heritage of every child of God, every son and daughter of the Father:

Just remaining quietly in the presence of God, listening to him, being attentive to him, requires a lot of courage and know how. This discipline of listening and of attention is a very high form of ascetic discipline, a rather difficult one to maintain....In this listening, in the tranquil attention to God, God acts directly upon the one who prays, doing it by himself, communicating himself to the soul, without other means, without passing through angels, men, images or forms....God and the beloved are together in great intimacy (*Contemplation in a World of Action*, pp. 363f).

Yet at the end of this journey of faith and love which brings us into the depths of our own being and releases us that we may voyage beyond ourselves to God, the mystical life culminates in an experience of the presence of God that is beyond all description and which is only possible because the soul had been completely "transformed in God" so as to become, so to speak, "one spirit" with him. Yet it is nothing else but the message of Christ calling us to awaken us from sleep, to return from exile, and find our true selves within ourselves, in the inner sanctuary which is his temple and his heaven, and (at the end of the prodigal's homecoming journey) the "Father's house" ("The Inner Experience," *Cistercian Studies* 18:14f).

It is not surprising, then, to find Merton insisting that the contemplative experience—contemplative prayer—is meant for all and not for a chosen few:

I have not only repeated the affirmation that contemplation is real, but I have insisted on its simplicity, sobriety, humility, and its integration in *normal Christian life*. This is what needs to be stressed....It is surely legitimate for anyone to desire and to seek this fulfillment, this experience of reality, this entrance into truth (*ibid.* 19:145f—Merton's italics).

Necessary Dispositions

As we have seen, Merton does call for certain dispositions in order to enter into this contemplative experience, into the Center. There must be a certain willingness to deny oneself at the more superficial levels and to live by faith, even a dark faith:

> According to the Christian mystical tradition, one cannot find one's inner center and know God there as long as one is involved in the preoccupations and desires of the outward self. Freedom to enter the inner sanctuary of our being is denied to those who are held back by dependence on self—gratification and sense satisfaction, whether it be a matter of pleasure-seeking, love of comfort, a proneness to anger, self-assertion, pride, vanity, greed, and all the rest. Faith...simultaneously a turning to God and a turning away from God's creatures—a blocking out of the visible in order to see the invisible. The two ideas are inseparable....But it is important to remember that the mere blocking out of sensible things is not faith, and will not serve as a means to bring faith into existence. It is the other way around. Faith is a light of such supreme brilliance that it dazzles the mind and darkens all its vision of other realities: but in the end, when we become used to the new light, we gain a new view of all reality transfigured and elevated in the light itself (*ibid.* 18:12f).

As we noted above in sharing Merton's dream, this faith needs to be nurtured by contact with the sources of Scripture and Tradition. It is the traditional way of *lectio, meditatio, oratio, contemplatio*—sacred reading, meditation, and prayer leading to contemplation. Merton explains this progression:

> Reading becomes contemplation when, instead of reason, we abandon the sequence of the author's thoughts in order not only to follow our own thoughts (medita-

tion) but simply *to rise above thought and penetrate into the mystery of truth which is expressed intuitively as present and actual.* We meditate with our mind, which is "part of" our being. But we contemplate with our whole being and not just with one of its parts (*ibid.* 18:291— Merton's italics).

This leads to one of the obstacles we can encounter as we move into Centering Prayer. We need to nourish our faith, the source of our Prayer, by faith reading. At the same time, however, we cannot cling to the concepts of faith that have nourished us, but must let them go in order to enter into the experience of faith through love. Faith leads us into the cloud of unknowing, and it is there, and there alone, in this life that we can immediately encounter the living God.

> In fact, the spirit sees God precisely by understanding that he is utterly invisible to it. In this sudden, deep, and total acceptance of his invisibility, it casts far from it every last trace of conceptual meditation, and in so doing, rids itself of the spiritual obstacles which stand between it and God. Thoughts, natural light, and spiritual images are, so to speak, veils or coverings that impede the direct, naked sensitivity by which the spirit touches the Divine Being. When the veils are removed, then I can touch, or rather be touched by, God in the mystical darkness. Intuition reaches him by one final leap beyond itself, and ecstasy by which it sacrifices itself and yields itself to his transcendent presence. In this last ecstatic act of "unknowing" the gap between our spirit as subject and God as object is finally closed, and in the embrace of mystical love we know that we and he are one (*ibid.* 18:300).

To Truly Seek God

Another possible obstacle is that we begin to seek the experience of God rather than the God of experience or the God to be experienced:

> ...the problem is that of taking one's subjective experience so seriously that it becomes more important than the soul, more important than God. Our spiritual experience becomes objectified, it turns into an idol. It becomes a "thing," a "reality" which we serve. We are not created for the service of any "thing," but for the service of God alone, who is not and cannot be a "thing." To serve him who is no "object" is freedom. To live for spiritual experience is slavery, and such slavery makes the contemplative life just as secular (though in a more subtle way) as the service of any other "thing," no matter how base: money, pleasures, success (*ibid.* 19:139).

When we start to seek an experience for ourselves, we are no longer seeking God, we are no longer centered on God but on self.

> If we remain in our ego, clenched upon ourselves, trying to draw down to ourselves gifts which we then incorporate in our own limited selfish life, then prayer does remain servile. Servility has its roots in self-serving. Servility, in a strange way, really consists in trying to make God serve our own needs. We have to try to say to modern man something about the fact that authentic prayer enables us to emerge from our servility into freedom in God, because it no longer strives to manipulate him by superstitious "deals" (*Contemplation in a World of Action*, p. 334).

We find here a very subtle balance between seeking for self and a due expectation, for love of its very nature does want union with the Beloved. The key lies here: the seeking is really a response, the response of love, the desire that love is.

> ...one of the basic rules is that it is always a gift of God. It is always something for which we must learn how to wait. But it is also something which we must learn to *expect actively*. The secret of the contemplative life is in this *ability for active awareness*, an active and expectant awareness where the activity is a deep personal response on the level which is, so to speak, beyond the faculties of the soul (*Contemplation in a World of Action*, p. 341—Merton's italics).

Self, then, selfishness, self-centeredness is the obstacle to Centering, to being Centered in God. It is the very antithesis to being to God in love, to God, and therefore necessarily to others, for they are in him.

> No man who ignores the rights and needs of others can hope to walk in the light of contemplation, because his way has turned aside from truth, from compassion, and therefore from God. The obstacle is in our "self," that is to say in the tenacious need to maintain our separate, external, egocentric will (*New Seeds of Contemplation*, pp. 18ff).

The Effects of Centering Prayer

The effect of contemplation, of Centering Prayer, is just the opposite:

> Rightly accepted, contemplative experience has its own proper effect: it increases the intensity and simplicity of a man's love for God and for his fellow men ("The Inner Experience," *Cistercian Studies* 18:291).

This contemplative love leads to freedom and creativity:

> The nothingness within us—which is at the same time
> the place where our freedom springs into being—is
> secretly filled with the presence and light of God as
> long as our eyes are not on ourselves and then our
> freedom is united with the freedom of God himself.
> Nothing can impede the joy and creativity of our acts
> of love (*ibid.* 19:143).

Contemplative insight does not only reveal to us the absorbing
beauty of God and our own intrinsic beauty in him. It also
reveals to us the beauty of every other person, each of whom is
one with us in God. Merton speaks of his own experience here:

> It was as if I suddenly saw the secret beauty of their
> hearts, the depths of their hearts where neither sin,
> nor desire, nor self-knowledge can reach, the core of
> their reality, the person each one is in God's eyes. If
> only they could all see themselves as they really *are*. If
> only we could see each other that way all the time.
> There would be no more war, no more hatred, no more
> cruelty, no more greed… (*Conjectures of a Guilty By-
> stander*, p. 142—Merton's italics).

In a word, the fruits of Holy Spirit will be very present in our
lives when we live out of our contemplative experience. This is
surely the way we can judge the authenticity of our experience. Our contemplation should overflow into the whole of
our lives, creatively bringing a certain sacredness to our environment because our eyes have been open to the sacred that is
already there and we live and act accordingly.

> All around this centered solitude radiates a universe
> which meditates and prays, a universe outside the uni-
> verse….It creates a radiation, a sacred universe cre-
> ated by the presence of a man in this particular kind of

relation with God. And this is very important (unpublished journal, March 8, 1966).

Contemplation becomes then constant stance. It is spontaneous awe at the sacredness of life, of being. It is gratitude for being. It is a vivid realization of the fact that life and being in us proceed from an invisible, transcendent, and infinitely abundant Source...above all, awareness of the reality of the Source...the awareness and realization, even in some sense the experience, of what each Christian obscurely believes, "It is now no longer I that lives but Christ lives in me" (*New Seeds of Contemplation*, pp. 1ff).

From these few quotes we can readily see what a rich source we have in the writings of Thomas Merton to support our practice of Centering Prayer and to understand the Prayer better. Some of his books I find especially relevant to Centering Prayer: *New Seeds of Contemplation, Conjectures of a Guilty Bystander, Contemplation in a World of Action*, and "The Inner Experience." This last is an unfinished work which, according to the terms of Merton's legacy, cannot be published as a book. It has, however, been published serially in the review *Cistercian Studies Quaterly* in 1983 and 1984.

I would like to conclude this chapter with a prayer of Father Merton:

To be here with the silence of Sonship in my heart is to be a center in which all things converge upon you. That is surely enough for the time being. Therefore, Father, I beg you to keep me in this silence so that I may learn from it the word of your peace and the word of your mercy and the word of your gentleness to the world. And that through me perhaps your word of peace may make itself heard where it has not been possible for anyone to hear it for a long time (*Conjectures of a Guilty Bystander*, p. 161).

Transformation
of Consciousness

We do, indeed, want to enter into "the silence of Sonship" and find that "center in which all things converge." We want to move from self-consciousness to God-consciousness. We want to leave behind our self-centeredness and grow in an effective consciousness that God is the Center, our center, the center of all that is. We want to come to know Reality and live lives that are shaped by Reality and not by illusion, fabrication, and self-deceit.

This is what we mean by "transformation of consciousness." "Transformation"—a big word, but one easy to break down. The "-tion" implies a certain permanence in the state described. "Trans" implies a going over, a change of position: transport—to carry over; transfer—to take one's self to a different place; transition—coming into a different situation. So, "transformation" means changing the form of our consciousness, coming into a new state of consciousness. "Consciousness" is the way we perceive things, the context within which we hold them.

With a transformation of consciousness we come to see things differently. The change we want, of course, is to come to see things as they really are—to see them as God sees them.

In scriptural language, this is rebirth in Christ: "Unless one be born again one cannot enter into the Kingdom." This has happened to us essentially in baptism. We were buried with Christ in the waters. We died to ourselves—our false selves, the person of sin. And rose again, as we came up out of the waters, to a new life in Christ. I am happy that baptism by immersion is being restored to practice in the Catholic Church. It has always been held in some other Christian churches. It so much more fully brings out the meaning of the rite.

At baptism [let me note that when I say "baptism" I usually mean to include baptism of desire—the desire to do what is right as one perceives it—the means whereby the majority of the human family come into the order of grace] we are brought to a new level of being. We are made partakers of the divine life and nature. If we are to be integral, what has happened at the level of being has to be appropriated also at the level of consciousness. As divinized men and women, we need a God-like consciousness; we need to see things as God sees them if we are to act in accord with our renewed nature.

At our natural birth, our perception makes us the center of the universe, of all that is. We are a little bundle of potential, much in need, very conscious of our needs. That is our first consciousness: the things we need. (Soon enough we begin to confuse "what I need" and "what I want.")

As our consciousness begins to expand, we become aware of those persons who supply our needs: mother, father, family, and so on. The circle expands with the years.

In time, largely under the tutelage of these significant persons, we come to see what we do as being significant. "Mama won't love Johnny if he doesn't eat his spinach." (Why do we always pick on spinach—a perfectly good vegetable?) "Janie is Daddy's good little girl if she puts away her dolls."

There is something very important involved in this. A parent's love, if it is true to its nature, is wholly gratuitous. No matter what a child does, no matter how he or she acts, good parents will still love their child. In this they are a sacrament of God's love—that wholly gratuitous love that brought us from non-being into being and sustains us at every moment. When parents begin to say things like "Mama won't love Johnny if he doesn't eat his spinach," with all the other forms this can take, they are trading on their parental love. This love is the most precious thing the child has. It is being bartered for small gains—a birthright is traded for a bowl of porridge. The effect of this—which can and often does last a lifetime—is devastating. The message the child begins to receive is that he or she has to earn love. The other side of this is the message that we are not lovable in ourselves. It opens the door to all kinds of acting out to try to win the love which we feel fundamentally we do not deserve.

Because the parents are the first sacrament of God's love in a child's life, this attitude passes over into our understanding of God's love. We begin to think that we must in some way earn God's love, yet we can never, of ourselves, be worthy of it. The effect here is far worse. For such an understanding of divine love is a total profanation of it. Nothing can win God's love, for God is the source of all love and all that is to be loved. God's love is absolutely gratuitous. It is so great it makes what it loves worthy of the love it receives. The effect of this false understanding of God's love is also more paralyzing. We know we can fool some people at least some of the time. We can hide from them that unlovableness of which we are convinced and by external performance—provided we don't let them get too close—we can win some kind of love, or at least some respect and friendship which will soothe the loneliness of our lives. But there is no fooling God. God knows us through and through. God knows fully our unlovableness. How can we win God's love? The answer to this false question has led to all sorts of aberrations. Many have not tried to answer it. They have just shut God out of their lives as someone they can't deal with.

I would certainly urge parents, especially parents of younger children, never to trade off the infinitely precious commodity of their parental love for some temporary gains. It is not worth it. The cost in the end can be astronomical. It can cost everything. Every child needs all the security and love he or she can possibly get.

But to get back to our evolution of consciousness—although all we have just said is certainly not aside from this consideration—as we grow we tend, largely because of the way others mirror us back to ourselves, to identify ourselves with what we have, what others think of us and what we can do. We tend to construct a false self made up of these elements: what we have, what we do, what others think of us. This becomes the way we think of ourselves and present ourselves to others.

Edmund White, in one of his novels, portrays this in all its adolescent nakedness. He records a boy's jealous thoughts about the basketball hero: "Being popular was equivalent to becoming a character, perhaps even a person, since if to be is to be perceived, then to be perceived by many eyes and with envy, interest, respect, or affection is to exist more densely, more articulately, every last detail minutely observed and thereby richly rendered."

Reflect just a moment. How often when a man introduces himself does he not immediately add what he does—or gives you his business card. "I am Joe Jones. I work at Sperry's." "I am Phil Donovan. I am a professor over at C.U." Women do not tend to do this so much. Perhaps it is because, up until recently, what most of them were doing—homemaking—was not held in particular regard; was not perceived as adding anything to their identity. But they perhaps made up for this lack of doing by the display of what they had. It is only now men seem to be catching up with women in wearing their gold and silver and gems. The right car, the right address, the right club are seen as significant. And what about name-droppers?

If in this reflection we have been thinking mostly of others, we might do well to come home and look at ourselves on these points. Even monks, priests, and religious.

We can immediately see the consequences of such a false self-identification. When we create such a false self, we have created a very, very fragile self. The true self, the inner man, is experienced not at all, or only as something hollow. We depend wholly on what is without for our meaning and existence. And it can so easily be lost. Thomas Merton wrote of this in *The New Man*, his finest and deepest theological work:

Why must we live in the shadow-kingdom of beings who can never quite believe that they themselves exist? Without the living God (without a center) men become little helpless gods, imprisoned within the four walls of their own weakness and fear. They are so conscious of their weakness that they think they can only subsist by snatching from others the little that they have, a little love, a little knowledge, a little power.

Recently I saw a grown man almost cry when he lost a glove. It wasn't that the glove was particularly special. It was just that he had so identified himself with what he had that it was a part of himself that was lost. We can find ourselves seriously betraying ourselves to please others, because the false self lives in their estimation of us. This is one of the reasons why loneliness is so devastating. In the moment we perceive no one is thinking of us and caring for us, we seem to cease to exist. When we can no longer do the things we have been doing, we are demolished. Isn't this the sad story of many men at retirement? For forty years or more they have said, "I am Joe, who works at Sperry's. I am Phil who teaches." What are they going to say now? An identity is lost—and all too frequently a life. This kind of self-identification has made it very difficult for some priests to accept the changes in the evolving Church. Many of the functions and duties with which they identified have been taken on by others: married deacons, eucharistic ministers, parish and financial councils, charismatic teachers.... Little is left but the essential, with which they all too little identified in the past, at least in a practical way.

Because such a construct—this false self made up of what I have, what I do, and what others think—is so fragile, it leads to a great deal of defensiveness. We have to protect who we are. An open generosity is much too risky, unless it is essential to keep people thinking well of us. Because what we have, and what we can accomplish, and what others think of us can be limited by what others do, a real competitiveness comes into our lives. We cannot rejoice over others' good fortune—it might result in their getting some of the acclaim we would get, or their getting ahead to our detriment. We tend to try to get ahead stepping on other people's heads.

If we have had a religious upbringing, then God tends to show up in this, also. He becomes the person out there whom we most need to think well of us. He is the one we most want to satisfy by doing the right things. It is from him we hope to get the real goodies, the ones that last forever. We have reduced God to our level—a real idol, not the true God.

GOD

One of the effects of all this is a deep resentment. To get what I want I have to do what all these others want, what God wants. I cannot do what I want and get what I want. So we resent people, and even God. We probably are not too conscious of this: after all, we are trying to please these people so that they will think well of us. We cannot let our resentment out. In fact, we dare not even let ourselves be in touch with it, for it would make our task of pleasing these people too difficult. We have to hold that we like these people, even as they truncate our freedom to be. Such suppressed resentment is dangerous. I believe it is at the root of much of the anger and hostility that is so frequently erupting in our society. When we cannot act against those whom we really resent, the suppressed resentment—unless we find some way to dissipate it—will eventually erupt chaotically and without direction. Even the most innocent become its victims.

What then are we to do? We need to realize—and even to know by experience—that God is not out there somewhere as the Great Rewarder or Punisher. I can remember from my early days a stained-glass window. It depicted a triangle with a great Seeing Eye in the middle of it. God was keeping an eye on me. Our God is out there—he is everywhere. And he does see everything—with his eye of love. But where is his favorite dwelling place on earth, in all creation? Where does he most immediately and significantly touch us and our lives? "The Kingdom of God is within." It is within us that the Father and the Son and their Holy Spirit have chosen to make their dwelling.

The shift of consciousness, the transformation of consciousness that we want, is to come to realize and to know by experience that God does dwell within us, with all his creative love, ever bringing us forth in his love and goodness. There is nothing we did, can do, or ever will do to earn this constant presence of affirming, caring, creating love.

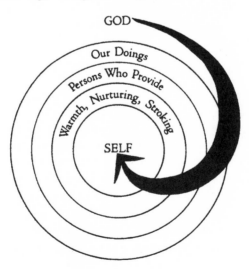

When we come to realize that God himself is ever with us, affirming our beauty, goodness, and significance by constantly sharing with us something of his own divine being and beauty, how can we care what others think—those who know us so much less. If you don't appreciate me, you are missing the boat. God does! With this transformation of consciousness which puts God experientially at the Center we are born to a new freedom. Or rather, we take possession of that freedom that was given to us in our rebirth in Christ, the Son in whom the Father is well pleased.

I no longer depend on what others think, on what I have, or on what I do for my identity or my worth. That stands of itself. It is. And it is in God. As Cardinal Law said in the interview he gave in the Vatican Gardens immediately after receiving the red biretta: "When God is seen at the Center, the human person is given a dignity, a respect, and a worth that no other system can give."

We come to know ourselves really only in the eyes of someone who loves us. That is one of the reasons why a first love is so special. For the first time (parents and family just have to love us, so that doesn't really count) someone has chosen us out of the multitude and gives us the gift of worshipful love. Love gives the lover added insight into our true beauty, and she or he reflects that back to us. What a wonderful experience! It is only God who can love us enough, whose eyes are big enough, to reflect back to us the whole of our beauty, for we are made in the very image of God. There is something infinite about us and infinitely beautiful.

Coming to know that we have within us the creative Source of all that is, we no longer need to be concerned about what we have. He has said, "Ask and you shall receive." We can have everything we want. And with his creative energy we can do all we want to do. We can create the kind of supportive relationships we want to create through the flow of such love. Life is extremely full.

We no longer need to be defensive. "Who can separate us from the love of God which is in Christ Jesus?"—for we are in

Christ Jesus. And therefore who can separate us from the abundant Source of all created goods? We begin to understand from within the teaching of our Lord in the Sermon on the Mount: "Your heavenly Father knows. Set your heart on his kingdom first, and on his righteousness, and all the other things will be given you as well." There is no need to compete. If we live out of our fullness, we will have more than enough. And so can everyone else. We begin to live out of a context of abundance rather than out of one of scarcity.

How can we bring about this transformation of consciousness?

Obviously, we cannot bring it about ourselves. We can only seek it and use our freedom to open the space for God to operate in us. For theory to become reality, a living reality in our lives, the Lord must reveal himself to us at the Center of our being. Through the activity of God's Spirit in the gifts, of which we have already spoken, we come to an experiential perception of Reality. A practical way to seek this transformation and open the space for God is to Center regularly. Centering Payer begins in seeking, continues in experiencing, and results in transformation. Only the fruit of that experience of God which makes us sensitive and perceptive of God's presence will enable us to live with a new consciousness, a God-consciousness, a consciousness that begins to see things as God sees them.

I would, though, like to suggest a practical little exercise which will help you realize something of what we are talking about. It is only those who have had the experience who understand, and those who have not had the experience need to seek the experience—then they will understand.

This exercise is very simple. Take a big sheet of paper, and print in large letters across the top of it, more or less evenly spaced, three words: DOINGS—PERSONS—THINGS. Then under "Doings" list the significant things you are doing; under "Persons," the significant persons in your life; and under "Things," the significant things you have. To give you and example, I might do it this way:

DOINGS	PERSONS	THINGS
praying	my community	my Bible
writing	my brother Dale	my cell
teaching	my brother Tommy	my office
gardening	my friend Ben	my word processor

—and so forth. Make your list as complete as you can.

Once you have made your inventory, cross off the first item under "doing" and imagine your life without it. Then the second: What would your life be without it? Then, the third. And so on down your list. When you have crossed out all the "doings," move on to the "persons" and eliminate them one at a time, looking at what is left of your life without them. Then move on to the "things" and work through them till they are all gone. (It was only later, when I was editing this chapter, that I realized I had affixed "my" to all the persons and things in my example. Did you? What does that tell us?)

At this point take another look at your life and list the doings, persons, and things you missed the first time. And then work your way through them, eliminating them one by one. Take another look. Maybe there are some more to list. Continue the process until the end. Then what do you have? Or, we might ask: Who are you? We will examine this question a bit further in the next chapter.

Pure Consciousness

In the last chapter we spoke about a transformation of consciousness. This transformation brings about a radical shift in our awareness and approach to life, to God, and to all others. We move from self-centeredness to God-centeredness—or perhaps it might be more correct to say we move through self-centeredness to God-centeredness. As Merton has said, "It is by the door of the deep self that we enter into the spiritual knowledge of God." The shift is from outwardness to inwardness, from illusion to reality. We were centered in self, but not the true self, rather, in the illusion we had created, made up of things outside ourselves. Turning within, we find our true self, the most perfect image of God, which leads us into God who is there as our constant Source.

This is indeed a participation in the Paschal Mystery. It is a death and resurrection. We die to the false self and rise to a new life in Christ in God. This transformation is not instantaneous; at least not ordinarily—God is the master of his gifts and he can bring it about in us in an instant if he wishes. Rather, the journey usually involves a repeated dying and rising again through the years. Finally, there does come a time, after many little deaths and resurrections, when we seem to undergo the great death and come into an experience of life in God that never again leaves us. There is a constant, abiding joy and Presence, even in the midst of the toils, the pains, and the passions of this "vale of tears." After this, we perhaps suffer even more because of greater compassion and love and because of the contrast—knowing what can be if only we will all say a complete "yes" to God.

93

Even when we have attained this openness to God with the Spirit functioning freely in our lives through his gifts, producing her fruits, there is yet more. As John of the Cross says: "Although these movements of Holy Spirit are most efficacious in absorbing the soul in sublime glory, they do not do so completely until the time comes for it to depart the sphere of the air of this carnal life and enter into the center of the spirit of the perfect life in Christ" (*The Living Flame of Love*, 3, 10). There is still room for more growth, even in this life.

In the initial transformation of consciousness we come to an experiential knowledge of God dwelling at the Center of our being and indeed in all things. Or, more accurately, we come to know all things as coming forth from God. We know them and know them more fully in God, more than we used to know them in themselves as apart from God. Yet for the moment there remains a distinction or division in this knowledge and experience. An "I-Thou" relation continues to exist. We have attained a God-consciousness, but not yet unity-consciousness. We have not yet so entered into the divine experience that we come to know how much we are one with God—a oneness brought to a new level of intimacy and participation through our baptism into Christ.

At the supper on the night before he died Jesus poured out his heart in prayer to his Father. There he uttered an absolutely amazing prayer. He prayed: "That they may be one, Father, as you in me and I in you, that they may be one in us." Christ Jesus, our Lord, is praying that we might have a unity with him and the Father like the unity they have with each other. This is utterly beyond our comprehension.

We have been made in the image of God. We know that the Father and the Son are absolutely one. And yet there is the distinction of persons. Through our likeness to God we have been brought into a unity with God that is beyond any union we can conceive, yet we are not absorbed. We remain distinct persons, able to delight in the love of the Other—yet that love is experienced now as our own; indeed, it is only Love and nothing else. It is a unity of love and experience so intimate and so complete that we as the subject of the experience simply disappear. There is no consciousness *of*. There is no subject left in the consciousness to be conscious of. There is just wholly, simply, and purely consciousness. And that consciousness is God.

Merton tries to explain this (I say "tries" for it is admittedly impossible to describe or explain—we stammer and stutter and say words that we know do not really express what we are talking about. It is again the old "Those who have experienced this know what I am talking about, and those who haven't, have the experience and then you will"):

Underlying the subjective experience of the individual self there is the immediate experience of Being. This is totally different from an experience of self-consciousness. It is completely non-objective. It has in it none of the split and alienation that occurs when the subject becomes aware of itself as a quasi-object. The consciousness of Being...is an immediate experience that goes beyond reflexive awareness. It is not "consciousness of" but *pure consciousness*, in which the subject as such disappears (*Zen and the Birds of Appetite*).

This perfect union is not a fusion of natures but a unity of love and experience. The distinction between the soul and God is no longer experienced as a separation into subject and object when the soul is united to God (*Thomas Merton Reader*).

What Merton says here is incorporated in the Third Rule of Centering Prayer: "Whenever you become *aware* of anything, simply, gently return to the Lord." The Prayer is simply being with God in a union of love. It is a total presence. As soon as we become aware of ourselves as being to God, then a split occurs. We step out of ourselves, as it were; we become alienated from ourselves as we stand outside and see ourselves as an object: someone who is with God. So, too, is the awareness of anything else when we see ourselves as the subject of the awareness: I am aware. This "I" has become an object of perception; we are watching ourselves have an experience. We are divided within ourselves. We are projecting and identifying with an "I" who is not the true self. In this "I" we have become an alien to our true self.

In our old consciousness, where we identified ourselves as that false self made up of what we have, what we do, and what others think of us, we were in a state of constant and complete self-alienation. We were not at home with ourselves at all. As we turn within and begin to know our true self, this split begins to be healed. We are coming home. Yet the split is totally healed only when we are ourselves in pure consciousness and no longer see ourselves as an object apart from the knowing subject. This self-knowledge comes to fullness when we experience ourselves as one with God in God and God is known in pure consciousness rather than by some subject-object knowledge. There is unity and simplicity here beyond accurate description.

During the time that we abide in this state of consciousness love is complete. The whole mind, the whole heart, the whole soul, and the whole of our strength, of our being is oned with God in complete gift, in purest delight, in total fulfillment. This is a moment outside of time. It is timeless. It is in the divine. It is a passage into the eternal NOW of God.

When we return to ordinary, everyday consciousness, we cannot report to ourselves what occurred, for there was no reflexive consciousness watching and recording; there was no object of which we were conscious. There was only pure consciousness. We can be conscious of the effects in our lives: integration, peace, tranquillity, centeredness, a sense of well-being and worth. We cannot rationally deduce the cause of all this, the reason for it, the source of this sense; we just know it is. Theology partially explains why these qualities flow from such an experience. We have looked at some of them in a previous chapter. The growth of these qualities in our lives is a good sign of the reality of our experience. We can judge a tree by its fruit—and need to—when the experience itself is beyond what we can judge with our rational mind or everyday consciousness, which is always a consciousness of something.

This experience is usually brief in time and, for most of us, all too infrequent. But having experienced it but once, even after many years of seeking it, the whole of our being says: It is worth it. Worth all the hours of sitting in the darkness, being purified, cleansed and prepared, our desire ever growing. Even if it never occurs again, our whole life would be worth it. Yet if we are faithful it will occur again and again, with the frequency that God knows is good for us. All praise to him, the All—Merciful and Good.

For Christians, our progression toward this experience of unity not infrequently passes through certain stages. In the beginning of our Prayer, Christ, the Way, the Truth, and the Life, may well be the Center of our Prayer. Our prayer word, or love word, may well reflect this. It may be a name or a title that belongs to the Son of Man: Jesus or Lord or Master or Savior or....Then, after a time, we come into such a unity with Jesus, the Lord and Son, that there is a shift in our consciousness. We come into an experiential oneness with the Son and are one with him to the Father in Holy Spirit. At this point our word may well change to Father or that word used by our Lord himself: Abba. We are no longer conscious of the Son, our Lord Jesus; our relation with him is one of pure consciousness or subjective identification. We have entered in some way into the inner consciousness of the Trinity, sharing the Son's relation to his Father in Holy Spirit. Christ's priestly prayer at the Last Supper is being fulfilled in us.

This shift of consciousness can be disturbing. For some, it proves a stumbling block. Jesus, the Way, the Truth, and the Life—our Way—seems to have disappeared from our Prayer. Did not that great Doctor of the Church, Teresa of Jesus, the mystic of Ávila, in her *Life*, argue strongly that we must always keep the Sacred Humanity present in our Prayer?

I can be totally sympathetic with this questioning and concern. I had been bred on Dom Columba Marmion: *Christ the*

Life of the Soul, Christ in His Mysteries, Christ the Ideal of the Monk. My first spiritual father was deeply nurtured in this Christological approach and strongly encouraged me in it. Yet the time came when Christ did seem to fade from my prayer, and I sensed it was time to change my prayer word from "Jesus," which I had used for many years, to "Father."

The question came up in our theology class. At that time we had an eminent Dominican professor who had come to us from the Pontifical University of St. Thomas Aquinas in Rome. As the question was debated he quoted to us Saint Paul: "If we once knew Christ in the flesh, we know him thus no longer." Then he brought forth the witness of our own holy Father, Saint Bernard of Clairvaux:

> Afterwards Jesus showed them a higher degree of love when he said, "It is the Spirit who gives life, the flesh profits nothing." I think Paul had reached this level when he said: "Even if we once knew Christ in the body, we know him thus no longer." Perhaps this was also true of the Prophet who said: "A Spirit before our face is Christ the Lord." When he adds: "Under his shadow we will live among the heathens," he seems to me to speak on behalf of the beginners, in order that they may at least rest in the shade since they know they are not strong enough to bear the heat of the sun. They may be nourished by the sweetness of his humanity since they are not yet able to perceive the things which are of the Spirit of God....Therefore in this human devotion there is in the meantime consolation for whoever does not yet have the Spirit which gives life, at least who do not have him in the same way as those who say: "A Spirit before our face is Christ the Lord," and again: "If we once knew Christ in the flesh we know him thus no longer." ...Of course, this devotion to the humanity of Christ is a gift, a great gift of the Spirit. I have called it carnal with comparison to that other love which does not know the Word as flesh so

much as the Word as wisdom, as justice, truth, holiness, loyalty, strength, and whatever else could be said in this manner. Christ is truly all of these (*Sermons on the Song of Songs*, 20:7f).

I had to let go of my "carnal devotion" and let the Spirit, Jesus' Spirit, lead me where he willed.

In this matter, I think Saint Teresa needs to be read with care and completeness.

In the twenty-second chapter of her *Life*, a place she refers back to in her later treatment of the question in the Sixth Mansion of her *Interior Castle*, the saint does offer a description of prayer that can be applied to Centering Prayer, with this caution: in Centering Prayer we never try to put aside images—rather, we seek to attend fully to the Lord in himself dwelling at the Center of our being. As we turn our attention to him it happens that we can no longer attend to anything else.

Of those who teach imageless prayer the saint says: "I do not contradict this view, for it is held by learned and spiritual men [such as Abba Isaac, Saint John Cassian, Saint Bernard of Clairvaux, the author of *The Cloud of Unknowing*, etc.], who know what they are saying, and God leads souls along many roads and by many ways, as he has led mine."

The saint also says of imageless prayer: "It will be all right to do this sometimes, but I cannot bear the idea that we must withdraw ourselves entirely from Christ and treat that divine body of his as though it were on a level with our miseries and with all created things." Anyone who practices Centering Prayer normally leaves images behind only during the actual time of the Prayer. At other times we do turn our attention to our Lord in his Sacred Humanity, above all at Mass and Communion. In any case, we never withdraw ourselves from Christ—we are intimately one with him through grace and baptism and depend wholly on him and pray through, with, and in him, so intimately that we are no longer conscious of him as apart from ourselves or of ourselves as apart from him. In our unity we are as it were one with him to the Father.

As the saint sets forth her teaching she says: "It is of mine that I now wish to speak, without interfering with the souls of others, and of the danger in which I found myself through trying to fall in line with what I read." Note here, the saint is but speaking of her own experience and not laying down norms for others. Moreover, she gives an example of how we can go off if we try to follow what someone—even Teresa—wrote rather than follow the way the Lord is leading us.

Later in the chapter the saint writes: "I have proved this [that prayer for her should always begin with consideration of the Sacred Humanity], for it is in this way that God has led my soul. Others, as I have said, will take another and a shorter road." That other and shorter road can be the way of Centering Prayer.

What the saint is most concerned about is that we will leave aside consideration of the Sacred Humanity out of pride, disdaining it as something less spiritual, or think some other form of prayer is superior and pursue it for that reason alone. Certainly to practice Centering Prayer or any form of prayer because of pride is wrong. But one can be led by the ordinary workings of grace to this kind of simple, contemplative prayer. The saint notes that it can be expected that God will so act in the soul "that, though we may not desire it to be so, this Presence of the Sacred Humanity is taken from us." And she goes on to counsel: "At such a time as that, let this be done. Blessed is such a loss, since it brings with it the enjoyment of more than we seem to have sacrificed; for the soul can then employ itself wholly in loving One whom the understanding has been striving hard to know; it loves what it has not comprehended and rejoices in that of which it could not have such great fruition save by losing itself, in order, as I say, the better to gain itself."

The need is to walk humbly each in our own way. If we feel called to meditate constantly on the Sacred Humanity, let us do so. If we wish to include a moment of consideration of our Lord in his humanity at the movement of faith at the beginning of Centering Prayer, let us do it. If we want to use the Holy Name of Jesus in our Centering Prayer, let us. If we have come to experience our profound oneness with Jesus and want only to be with him to the Father in the Spirit, let us do that, and let "Father" or "Abba" be our word, if that is the meaningful word for us. Let each follow the way in which he or she is being called.

When Saint Teresa was speaking of "learned and spiritual men" she may well have been thinking of her friend and Carmelite confrere, Saint John of the Cross. In his commentary on the third stanza of *The Living Flame of Love*, he gives much good advice that can be applied to Centering Prayer. Let me quote a bit from him:

When the appetite has been fed a bit and has become accustomed in a certain fashion to spiritual things and has acquired some fortitude and constancy, God begins to wean the soul, as they say, and place it in a state of contemplation. This occurs in some persons after a very short time....Since the soul cannot function naturally except by means of the senses, it is God who in this state is the agent and the soul is the receiver. The soul conducts itself only as the receiver and as one in whom something is being done; God is the giver and the one who works in it, by according spiritual goods in contemplation (which is knowledge and love together which is loving-knowledge), without the soul's natural acts and discursive reflections, for it can no longer engage in these acts as before....To make acts or strive for satisfaction and fervor, such activity would place an obstacle in the path of the principal agent who is God, who secretly and quietly inserts in the soul loving wisdom and knowledge, without specific acts....Thus the individual should proceed only with loving attention to God, without making specific acts. He should conduct himself passively, as we have

said, without efforts of his own, but with simple loving attentiveness, as a person who opens his eyes with
loving attention.

The saint leaves no room here for calling up images, even
of the Sacred Humanity or the Passion. He is, of course, speaking of one practicing this particular kind of prayer and not
laying down universal norms.

The saint develops his thought at length on this point (the
whole section is well worth reading—nos. 32ff in the Kava-
naugh-Rodriguez edition) and then goes after directors who
try to keep their subjects in the way of active meditation or
making explicit acts of devotion when the Lord is inviting them
to contemplation. Teresa would be included among these if
she had not nuanced her opinion the way she did, as does John
at the end of this passage:

> Since these spiritual directors do not understand what
> recollection and spiritual solitude is, nor its properties
> (in which solitude God pours these sublime unctions
> into the soul), they superimpose or interpose anoint-
> ing from a lower spiritual exercise, which is the soul's
> activity, as we said. There is as much difference be-
> tween what the soul does itself and what it receives
> from God as there is between human work and a di-
> vine work, between the natural and the supernatural.
> In the one God works supernaturally in the soul, in
> the other, the soul only works naturally. What is worse
> is that by the activity of his natural operation a person
> loses inner solitude and recollection and consequently
> the sublime image God was painting within him. Thus
> all his efforts are like hammering the horseshoe instead
> of the nail; on the one hand he does harm and on the
> other he receives no profit. These directors should re-
> flect that they themselves are not the chief agent, guide,
> and mover of souls in this matter, but that the princi-
> pal guide is Holy Spirit, who is never neglectful of souls,

and that they are instruments for directing them to perfection through faith and the law of God according to the spirit God gives each one. Thus the director's whole concern should not be to accommodate souls to his own method and condition, but he should observe the road along which God is leading them, and if he does not recognize it, he should leave them alone and not bother them (*The Living Flame of Love* 3, iii).

As we sit at the feet of the fathers and mothers, we must always remember that they are persons of their own times and that they each have their own particular call. They receive the living tradition, give their own particular expression to it, and then hand it on. Each one's contribution is something beautiful. Yet no one's is normative—the basic teaching of the living tradition remains the norm. Listening to the leading of the Spirit, we can choose the guides who help us most, we can choose the teaching that most supports the way in which we are being led.

In Athens there is a wonderful museum, the Museum of Icons. It has one of the largest collections of icons in the world. The thing I found most fascinating in this museum was the collection of festal or "great feast" icons. These icons may depict twelve to sixteen major feasts in the Christian year honoring events in the life of Jesus and Mary and also the coming of Holy Spirit. It has been the custom in Byzantine churches to mount a series of these icons on the icon screen at the front of the church and bring them down for the celebration of the particular feast. There are very precise canons or norms governing how each of these scenes is to be depicted. The large collection in the museum was fascinating because each of the many artists remained religiously faithful to the norms yet brought to his work his own particular gift. It was a powerful expression of a living tradition. The essentials were always there in each artist's series; but so were the differences. Sometimes these were very pronounced, sometimes they were very subtle, almost purely spiritual—and the latter were the most powerful.

The tradition of contemplative prayer in the Church lives. It has flowed through many hearts from the Heart of Christ. It will continue to flow. It will always be Christian—the pray-er identified with Christ. The deeper this identification, the more subtle it will be and the more powerful.

Recently a priest shared this experience. He had begun to practice the Prayer over thirty years ago. At first his prayer word was "Jesus." After about twelve years he realized that he had to change his word to "Father." A few weeks before his sharing, it became clear to him he must change his word again. This time he was invited to use the word "Pa." During those first weeks, each time he used this new prayer word he would totally dissolve into tears—that the Father should invite him into such intimacy and familiarity.

If he remains faithful, in all likelihood there will come a time when even this word of intimate love will lose its meaningfulness and slip away from him. He will enter into the silence of God in perfect unity.

In sharing all of this I want to underline once again: we must come to Centering Prayer with *no* expectations, no preconceived ideas about how it should develop. We should never try to force it. Rather, with the great reverence that flows out of love, we will totally respect the freedom of the other Party. We will give ourselves totally to him and let him do what he wants when he wants. If we do this we have the consoling assurance of Saint John of the Cross:

> It is impossible that God fail to do his part by communicating himself to the soul, at least silently and secretly.
>
> It is more impossible than it would be for the sun not to shine on clear and uncluttered ground. As the sun rises in the morning and shines upon your house so that its light may enter if you open the shutters, so God, who is watching over Israel and does not doze nor still less sleep, will enter the soul that is empty and fill it with divine goods.

Do not get caught up in trying to see the evolution in your Prayer. If you do, there will be no evolution. Live it, do not watch it. The greatest enemy of Centering Prayer is the "monitor," that part of us that wants to keep track of everything we do, just to be sure we are always right. It puts us squarely back into the center of the false self, the doing self. It is an agent of alienation and split. It creates a false self-centeredness. When we are Centered in God, the true Center, we find all. We find our own true self in all its beauty. We know there is but one Center and we are in that Center and of that Center. We become truly one with Christ, cosmic persons.

The Cosmic Person

Father John Main spoke of entering "into the experience of being swept out of ourselves, beyond ourselves, into this wonderful prayer of Jesus—this great cosmic river of love." Behind the poetry of this statement there is reality. As we enter more and more fully into unity-consciousness, pure consciousness—into possession of our oneness with Christ in God—we come to possess more and more the mind of Christ, the heart of Christ. We come to know more and more our oneness with all in the creating love of God, a oneness enhanced by the grace of the re-creation in Christ. The whole cosmos rests ever in the creating love of God, and we come to know, in our oneness with the Divine, that it rests within us to be held in infinitely tender love. We are one with the All and with all.

Two major systems confront each other in the struggle for possession of the earth: on the one hand, a democracy that glorifies the individual, and, on the other, a materialistic communism that reduces the individual to a collective, a crowd. Neither respects the reality that the individual is part of a whole. A person can only exist in relationship. Individualism encourages each cell of society to think of itself as its own center—very much like a cancer. Its relationship with others is accidental rather than organic. Materialistic communism would reduce these individuals to a soulless collectivity, a crowd or mass without a soul.

The soul of the human family is Holy Spirit—the Love of the Father for the Son and the Son for the Father—given as gift and poured out on all creation as a cosmic River of Love. It is this Love that is the bond of our unity.

The human person is and ever will remain distinct, unique, loving, and loved. Yet we are brought by creating Love into a unity that is beyond our comprehension—an image of the Trinity: one God, with an absolute oneness, yet ever three loving and loved Persons.

As we enter more and more into the experience of our true self in God, we come to sense the reality of this unity long before we can begin to understand it. To be true to ourselves we realize that we must live and act in such a way as to promote the spiritual unity of the world. We have to seek to "unite all the positive values of civilization in a totality which will also respect the individual values.... [We should seek to] attain that higher passionate unity in which we shall find rooted and consummated in a new synthesis the democratic sense of the rights of the person and the communistic vision of the potentialities contained in matter" (Teilhard de Chardin). Or better, a unity founded on the Church's sacramental reverence for the material, her profound respect for the individual person redeemed by Christ and her sense of the whole as the one Body of the cosmic Lord. We realize that the function of the human person is to build and direct the whole of the earth not out of fear of perishing but with an ambition for a fuller life—"I have come that they may have life and have it more abundantly"—not out of a sense of scarcity but out of the richness of our abundance.

We are called to be active participants with full responsibility for creating with God under God a "new heaven and a new earth." To do this we certainly need engineers occupied in organizing the resources of the earth and its lines of communication, enabling these resources to be used equitably for the well-being of every citizen of the earth. Alongside these, though, we need other "technicians" who will be concerned with defining and propagating the concrete goals, ever more lofty, upon which the efforts of our human activities should be concentrated. Where will this new "technology" essential to the well-being of a human world come from? From among those enlightened by the Spirit through the activity of his gift—truly

Centered persons. From them will evolve an understanding of the "psychic currents of attraction, a science of spiritual energy."

It has been interesting to watch the evolution of the United Nations. In its first years the meetings were almost totally concerned with political and economic accords. Then there began to emerge a need to formulate ethical codes which would undergird these accords. It has only been in recent years that the members have begun to speak, at times, of the affective attitude—they were not yet ready to speak openly of love—that must exist among peoples if the ethical codes are to succeed in binding the human family together in a life-creating political and economic unity. Sad to say, all of this is again and again threatened by blatant nationalism and greedy materialism and the antithesis of love: war and all those forms of violence which destroy human life and spirit.

Faced with the enormous forces that are at play on the world scene—at the level of the United Nations, summit meetings, and areas of aggression—what can the individual person do? That question confronts each one of us who has the courage not to resort to some numbing drug to avoid it. The question itself could leave us numb, paralyzed with fear and a complete sense of helplessness. It is only if we have a real sense, flowing from inner experience, that the power which has created this universe is in some way ours to wield that we can abide in a peaceful and even joyful belief that our lives can make a difference, that there is "hope for the daisies."

In touch with the Center, we know that at every moment the whole of this creation comes forth from a creating Love. Its course can be radically altered at any moment in that sequence which we call time. And, however tortuous its course may be through time, it will come to completeness in that new heaven and new earth which already exist in the eternal NOW of creative Love. Furthermore, we know that, by the mysterious designs of that Love, how the earth will be brought forth in the next moment, the next hour, the next day, and the next year will in some part be determined by our will. For he has said, "Ask and you shall receive." The prayer of the faithful is infinitely powerful because it harnesses all the power of the Infinite.

But the God of Love does not listen to the lisping of human lips. God hears only the beating of human hearts and what rests within them. It is the compassion that comes out of the experience of oneness and holds the world in infinitely tender love that speaks efficaciously to the divine creative Love and alters the course of history. It is not some beautiful thought or insightful idea, but being with the groanings of the earth and all its peoples that makes our prayer.

It is not, then, ideas that are going to make us effective cosmic persons able to make a real difference in the redeeming of the earth: it is only living out of the Center of Unity and Oneness. Richard Heckler in his *Anatomy of Change* says, "The state of Center is a doorway, a place to begin feeling our deeper urges, our possibilities in the world, the expansiveness of our excitement, and also our need to be nourished in quiet contained ways." Heckler speaks from another tradition but I like the way he expresses the idea. Merton would speak of Centering Prayer bringing us to the ground of being. This grounding keeps us out of our heads and makes things tangible and real. It allows us to respond from a grounded, secure sense of who we are. Rather than experiencing confrontation and conflict, we flow in harmony with the forces of the universe and enter and blend with the forces around us. This entering and blending is so loving that it creates a change of context, a shift from the expectation of harm to the probability of harmony. Blending creates an alternative to having winners and losers in confrontational situations. It allows us to work with others where they are, rather than from a preprogrammed moral or judging place. Rather than reacting, we move with the incoming energies—even when they are attacking or when they are an obstacle—and experience them as they are, moving with them and working with them in a creative way. By making ourselves vulnerable in this way we are truly compassionate; we are one with the other and gain power over the direction of change. Understanding this, we are open to all sorts of possibilities.

Coming from the Center, knowing happens from the inside out: we know things from within. We know the essential goodness of all that is and we know that destructive forces come only from misdirection and truncation. To bring redirection and fullness lies within our creative potential if we live fully in the present moment as one with all that is.

Joy, insight, and success are most accessible when we live in the present, one with the present. Fear and worry do not stand up to reality. They come from expectations which lie in a projected future that does not exist apart from our anticipation or from misperceptions which arise from seeing reality from without rather than from within. Figments of the mind and imagination are poor substitutes for true experience. They satisfy and nourish us just about as much as an imaginary meal or a picture or a definition of a meal would satisfy the stomach.

Immediate experience in the "now" in the Center enables us to hold the whole cosmos in compassionate love, knowing all its ills, and knowing its healing. We become part of that healing as our compassion becomes the efficacious prayer that "determines" the omnipotent, ever-creating Love. "If you remain in me and my words remain in you then you will ask for anything you want and you shall have it." "Words" here—*logoi*—doesn't just mean the recorded words of the Revelation. It means the whole creation in its truth. The *Logos*, the Word of God, rests in all creation, for it is by his word that all is made. If we remain in the Center, who is the God of creating Love, and we let all his words of creation rest in us, *then* will our prayer be totally efficacious.

The insistence here on the cosmic efficacy of our prayer, arising out of our identity with the cosmos, in no way wants to deny the importance of being present to the particular and the immediate. An expression or sense of cosmic compassion is an illusion if it is not effectively present in immediate action, where it can be in accord with our proper role in the human community. "How can you say you love God whom you cannot see, if you do not love your brother whom you can see?"

Our care for the cosmos will express itself first in reverent care for our own bodies, that piece of the cosmos which is our most special charge. Holiness is always holistic. The body is the temple of God: it must be kept with reverence and care. The body is the much needed servant of the spirit; it must be given all that it needs to serve well. Our care for our bodies, apart from a special call to sacrifice for a higher purpose, should dictate how we care for the bodies of others. Reverence calls for proper nutrition. It rules out overeating and junk eating as much as malnutrition. The concern carries over to our brothers and sisters. We are to love our neighbors as ourselves. We do what we can. Let me tell you of what one man has done, and in the doing called forth many others to be a part of the doing.

Deacon Carl Shelton of the Diocese of San Diego is a splendid example of what can be done with the dedication of some corporate know-how.

A man of exceptional charm and ability, Carl Shelton was very successfully climbing the corporate ladder. With his high level of dedication he could well have reached the very top and situated his family in the lap of luxury. But Carl began to take his discipleship of Jesus Christ seriously; through Centering Prayer his life became centered. He soon left the corporate scene and established a small business in San Diego which would enable him to get his sons through college, prepare for the diaconate, and discern how best to use his uncanny business sense for the Lord. After a month with Mother Teresa in Calcutta, Carl decided to do something about feeding the hungry. But as a true leader he had too much respect for his fellow humans to aim at a patronizing give-away program. Everyone has a right to help oneself.

SHARE (Self-Help and Resource Exchange) was born, and within a year it was sharing over a million pounds of food a month on this side of the border in San Diego and distributing larger and larger amounts among the poorest of the poor across the border, in San Diego's impoverished sister city of Tijuana.

Shelton's idea was simple but ingenious. He would get large

producers to sell him enormous quantities of foodstuffs at reduced prices. Those participating in the program would pay twelve dollars and contribute two hours to community service and in return would receive sixty to seventy pounds of mixed produce, which always includes meat, bread, vegetables, fruit, and staples. The two hours of service provided the labor force to handle the foodstuff, prepare and distribute the seventy-pound packages, do the office work, and distribute the give-away food to the totally impoverished.

Rather than creating a whole new organizational octopus, Carl networked many existing groups which he calls "host organizations." These local groups enroll the participants, collect their moneys, supervise their community service (up to 40 percent of which can be used by the local organization for its own ministries), and distribute the food packages. Others who do not need food assistance but want to be part of SHARE can be sponsors, providing funds for those who cannot afford even the twelve dollars and rendering services, like the many truckers who get the food to the distribution points. At the time of the monthly food distribution any one of these points and above all the main warehouse take on an almost carnival atmosphere, a hard-working one, as people help people and everybody profits. There are no racial, color, creedal, or even poverty requirements to participate in SHARE. Government handouts are not a part of SHARE's self-help program, but its donated community services do make it possible for SHARE to distribute large quantities of such foodstuffs gratis to the completely deprived on both sides of the border. SHARE is backed by the Diocese of San Diego and unites more than two hundred other organizations: schools, labor unions, housing associations, community groups, and churches of many traditions. It is truly ecumenical.

Shelton and his immediate collaborators have put in an immense amount of dedicated hours to make SHARE go. Carl went to Chicago. There with the support of his own bishop and the blessing of Cardinal Bernardin, he assisted local deacons to start a SHARE program there. That same month also saw the beginning of SHARE in Virginia. These were the first. SHARE has come to New York and to Newark. Carl hopes there will be many independent but mutually supportive SHARE groups in all parts of our blessed nation. There need not be a single hungry person in America—or in the world, for that matter—and there won't be if each of us lives out of the Center and does what he or she can to nourish our Body, the cosmic Body of Christ.

Most of us will not be able to produce such spectacular results or undertake a great enterprise like Deacon Shelton—though we should take care not to sell ourselves short. With God's help we can do even the unimaginable. Let us each bring the gifts we have and offer them generously and courageously to the service of the whole. And let God worry about the results. He does choose the weak things of this world to accomplish his mighty deeds.

Food is certainly a basic human need. But there are other needs we will be concerned about as well. The human body needs exercise—a real asceticism for many. The mind, too, needs exercise. Education and educational facilities for all are our concern. Even more important for us is the nourishment of the spirit: religious education and sacramental food, psychological care and friendship. When we come out of the Center our concern is lively on all levels of human well-being both for ourselves and for others.

We need a worthy environment for all of this. Even as the body is the gracious environment of the human spirit, so the body of the earth is the common shared milieu of human life. Our ecological concern can begin with some immediate and personal caring, such as not smoking and being careful in disposing of waste. It will grow to include cities and forests, farmlands and nature preserves, rivers and oceans, and nuclear waste and renewable energy sources. The little and the vast are all our concern. "You should do these first, while not laying aside the others."

It is our world. We are persons of the cosmos. We may not know in detail as much about it as we would like to, nor all that we can do to care for it. But we can hold it in love from the Center and believe in the wholing and healing power of creative Love. That love we can bring to all the earth and to every member of the human family. Anything less than that would not be worthy of us as being who we are—cosmic persons.

Ours for the Receiving

A question I am often asked when Centering Prayer is referred to as a "method of contemplative prayer" is: Can we force God to give us contemplative prayer? We have already spoken a little about this, but I think it is worth returning to the subject.

First of all, "a method of contemplative prayer" might not be the best way to describe Centering Prayer. There are many different notions of just what contemplative prayer is, the term being used to cover a broad spectrum of experiences. So we have decided to leave the label aside and stay with the title: Centering Prayer.

Surfacing in this question is a fear that has long been prevalent in our Church: the fear of Pelagianism. Pelagius was a fourth-century monk. Saint Augustine did much to bring his errors to the fore. They were finally condemned by a Church council. The essence of his error—or at least the error attributed to him—lay in the assertion that the human person can be the ultimate source of some good, unaided by grace. God and God alone is the ultimate source of all good. Whatever good is to be found in creation and in the human person has its sources in him.

Therefore we cannot pray, or pray as we ought, without God's grace.

And yet we know that we can decide right now to turn our attention from this book and say an Our Father. Try it and see. Stop reading for a moment and pray the Our Father.

⸎

Our Father,
who art in heaven
hallowed be your name.
Your kingdom come.
Your will be done
on earth as it is in heaven.
Give us this day
our daily bread.
Forgive us our trespasses
as we forgive those
who trespass against us.
Lead us not into temptation,
but deliver us from evil.
For yours is the kingdom,
the power,
and the glory
for ever and ever.
Amen.

We can only do what we have just done by God's grace; yet that grace is always available to us. God has commanded us to pray constantly. God backs up his commands with his grace.

There are two freedoms at play here: the freedom of God and our freedom. God has freely bound himself to give us the grace we need—indeed, the grace we ask for: "Ask and you shall receive." There yet remains our freedom to respond to his grace and use or abuse it. We are touching here one of the more difficult mysteries of our faith: the interplay of grace and free will. After exhaustive searching into the question—How is it that God's grace moves us to do good and yet we move freely?—Saint Augustine made this response to the question: "Do not seek an answer if you do not want to come up with a wrong answer." There are some answers we do not yet have. They will be revealed to us only when we are brought into the fullness of the Divine Mystery.

We do not have the answers because we do not need them. We do need faith and trust.

We can pray the Our Father. And we can decide to pray it in different ways. We can, as they say, "rattle it off" rather quickly. This is not necessarily a wrong way to use this prayer. It can be the vehicle of a very great love, sent to God express.

There is a story in our monastic tradition. One day the steward of a very wealthy lord arrived at the gate of a monastery with a large bag of gold as an offering for the monks. The steward's lord wanted the monks to pray for a deceased brother. Graciously accepting the sack, the monk at the gate turned toward the abbey church and prayed a short psalm, Psalm 128(129), the usual psalm for the deceased. He then turned back to the astonished steward and offered him a drink and other humanities. The steward blurted out: "Is that all you are going to do for such a generous offering?" The monk smiled and took the man into his cell. He sat at his desk for a minute or two and wrote out the psalm. Then he took his scales. He placed the bag of gold on one side and the sheet of paper with the psalm written on it on the other. The bag of gold shot up as the weight of the psalm bore down on the scale. "So are things weighed in God's eyes, my friend. And now, can I get you something to drink?"

It is the love that matters!

We can, though, decide to say the Our Father with very great care, letting our emotion and affection come into the words. This will take longer. And such a recitation may stir up and increase our love, or at least give better expression to it.

Again, we may decide to seek to enter into this Prayer more fully. The Lord gave it to us, not so much as a formula of prayer, but more as a whole school of prayer. We can meditate on each word and each phrase, applying our minds to them, drawing out all the implications we can. Saints have written whole books on the Lord's Prayer. Our reflections will undoubtedly lead us into praying more deeply the sentiments contained in the Prayer.

Finally, we may decide to open ourselves, and receive the Prayer contemplatively. We rest in the reality of Father—our Father. If we do this, and use the word Father to help us stay with that Reality in love, we will find ourselves quite "naturally" in Centering Prayer.

In a word, what I would like to say here is that anyone can enter into Centering Prayer. The grace and the freedom are ours. Yes, it is a gift. But the gift is given, it is ours for the taking.

Once an elderly nun asked Saint Teresa of Jesus: "Mother, how can I become a contemplative?" The saint, who is recognized as a Doctor of the Church—one of the great and authoritative teachers of prayer—replied: "Sister, say the Our Father, but take an hour to say it." The sister was invited to give God the space to show up in her life. That's where our freedom lies.

One day a monk who lived on the banks of the Nile asked his Father about the different kinds of prayer. The Father took him to the bank of the river and pointed out three monks on the water. One was rowing laboriously. The second was going with the current, plying the tiller to move in the direction he wished. The third had set a sail and was flying along. "Some pray with their minds, with the oars of thought and image. Their prayer is all work," said the Father. "Others pray with their hearts. Their prayer can be very sweet and enjoyable. But they must keep their hands on the tiller to keep on course or they may follow the movements of a heart not yet fully purified. And others open fully to the breath of Holy Spirit, who has been given to them as gift, and let him pray in them. As the holy Paul said: 'We do not know how to pray as we ought, but Holy Spirit prays within us.'"

The choice is really ours. The gifts have been given to all of us at baptism. We can open out to the breath of the Spirit and let her move us in a prayer that is wholly divine and fully worthy of the God to whom we pray. Or we can keep our sails furled, our gifts packed, and insist on using tiller or oars. God remains free in this, of course. The gifts are constantly given, coming forth from the freedom of God's creative love. The wind can cease to blow and our sails stand slack. But our just being there, open to it, is yet our part of the Prayer; the pure gift of ourselves to God. Even this giving on our part is God's gift, just as it is God who has given us the oars (reason and imagination) and the tiller (affections). The giftedness of prayer is perhaps most readily seen in the breath of contemplative prayer, the prayer of the Spirit in us. That is one of the reasons why the life of the gifts, the mystic life as some would call it, or the way of contemplative prayer, rather than puffing up the receiver with pride, fosters the basic virtue of humility. It makes it so obvious that all is gift.

Why, then, would one choose to row or ply the tiller rather than open the sails of contemplative prayer? Why do some find it difficult to accept the gift of the gifts and their activity in our lives?

There are many possible reasons.

Some of us like to remain in control, seeking to maintain a rather false and very limited autonomy. Who can be autonomous from God? Yet many are caught in the illusion of autonomy even as they use God's gifts of life and freedom.

Some of us are afraid to let go. We want the course to be chartered in advance, step by step. But: "Eye has not seen, nor ear heard, nor has it entered into the heart of the human person what God has prepared for those who love God." We need to trust the Love of God.

Others are really afraid to love—for, truth to tell, as free as love is, it is absolutely captivating. When we open ourselves and let the divine beauty invade our lives, we quickly come to know that we cannot live, or live happily, without it. Such a God of goodness and love, how can we ever offend God? We can only do what God wants. We are the slaves of love.

Some want always to be right. They sense a real need to be right. They do not yet know their true selves and are trapped in the construct of a false self, a part of which is doing what is right. In order to be sure they are doing what is right, the right way, they must ever keep an eye on themselves and all that they do. They can never let go and turn both eyes to God. They are anchored in the finite and so there is no room in them for the revelation of the Infinite.

Flowing from these reasons is the desire that some of us have to be able to pat ourselves on the back. We want to do things the hard way, to merit what we get, to earn our own way, to stand on our own two feet. But: "Unless you become as a little one, you cannot enter the kingdom"—the kingdom that is within.

In the end the only thing that matters with God is love. God is love. As John of the Cross has said, "In the evening of life, we will be judged on love." Love is the response of the heart to the good. When we open the space in our lives for God to show up we experience his goodness; then we grow mightily in love, for his goodness calls forth the greatest love. If we insist that God contract to fit within the limits of the concepts of our minds or the images of our imagination, our love will not greatly expand. Anything that our minds can master can hardly call us forth from ourselves in contemplation.

God's call to personal friendship is universal. When our

Lord said at the Last Supper, "I no longer call you servants because I have made known to you all that the Father has made known to me," he was speaking to all who receive his Revelation. And his command to his disciples was to "go forth and teach all nations." He stands knocking at the door of the heart of every human person. Though his guises are many and varied, his desire is always the same: to come in and sit down side by side with a beloved friend and sup with that friend, sharing a divine nourishment.

We know from our own experience the freedom of friendship. We decide to whom we will offer the gift of openness to the life sharing that is friendship. We know, too, the freedom of the other to respond or not respond. The Lord has clearly offered the gift of intimate friendship. The freedom lies with us to accept. The grace is there for us to accept, or the Lord's offer would be a charade. We all know that friendship must go beyond words and thoughts and feelings. It calls for the gift of self and the silences of such communication.

Centering Prayer is but responding to the offer of the intimacy of divine friendship. In the authenticity of the evangelical invitation, freely given, the grace is freely given to respond. If you want to call this response contemplation I do not think you would be wrong.

"...and I Will Refresh You"

The word "center" can be taken in two senses. It can be an active verb, and it is used in this sense in *The Cloud of Unknowing*: "Center all your attention and desire on him [God]...." It can also be taken in a passive sense as being a place. This is the way in which Merton used it: "A man cannot enter into the deepest center of himself and pass through that center into God unless he is able to pass entirely out of himself and empty himself and give himself to other people in the purity of selfless love." Incidentally, this statement affirms what we have tried to bring out in the chapter on the cosmic person: we cannot be Centered without that including an embrace of the whole cosmos, without coming into and accepting our responsibility of universal love. It is also an interesting text because, even as it speaks of "center" in the more passive sense, it affirms the powerful activity that must accompany this coming into the Center of all rest.

In our thinking we tend to see rest or leisure in direct contrast to work or activity. But this is not the reality. If it were, we could never speak of working leisurely or of restful activity.

The contrast really is in the give-and-take of life. Leisure, rest, recreation, come out of the balance between the giving and taking. Think of the human heart. A magnificent muscle, it never stops working; yet it is always restoring itself and the rest of the human body—at least so long as its basic rhythm of give-and-take is not impaired. It takes in blood and then gives it forth. It contracts, it relaxes. It works and it rests. The lungs carry on their endless task in a similar way.

The problem of life comes from the fact that we are a taking people, an aggressive people. We tend to take things in hand and close our pudgy little fists tightly around them. Not only do we take an exam, take a meal, take a left...but we even take things that should be restful: we take a seat, take a nap, take a break. We take, take, take until we can't take it anymore. And then, alas, we are apt to take our lives.

Note all the contradiction in this. To take one's life means exactly the opposite of what it says. The man who takes his life actually loses it. If we actually took a seat we would be carrying a chair around instead of sitting down to rest. We give ourselves to the chair, to the nap, to the rest. It is precisely because our inner disposition is not one of giving, but of taking, that the things that should balance our lives and give us rest do not. We make work out of them. We do them energetically, aggressively, always in control, not letting them minister to us.

There are basically two kinds of meditation or prayer: the effortful and the effortless. We find them both in the different traditions.

An example of the effortful would be the discursive meditation which has prevailed so strongly in our recent Catholic tradition. We work with some text from the gospels, for example, and seek to extract from it all we can, using our minds and our imaginations to the full, until finally we break through and experience the reality, and rest in it. As the breakthroughs do not always come, especially in the short time we usually allot to daily meditation, prayer is work. It leaves us still aggressively engaged. No wonder the Lord's words, "Come to me all you who labor and are heavily burdened and I will refresh you," do not ring true.

Rinzi Zen would be an example of this effortful approach from another tradition. The Zen master gives the disciple a koan—an enigmatic statement like "What is the sound of one hand clapping?"—and the disciple then proceeds to sit in a rigid, intense posture for hours, and sometimes days and years, exercising his wits on the question until suddenly he breaks through the rational mind and comes to the experience of the reality that is beyond it. Until the breakthrough there is little refreshment to be found in Rinzi Zen.

On the other hand, Transcendental Meditation, as taught by Maharishi Mahesh Yogi, would be an example of effortless meditation from an Eastern tradition. Here the meditator lets everything go and simply lets his sound mantra effortlessly repeat itself until the mind emerges into the fourth state of consciousness or transcendence.

In our own tradition we find Centering Prayer. We just let everything go and with a most gentle movement of the will enter into "the great cosmic river of love"—the prayer Jesus. We learn to let go and be and receive.

Meditation, or Centering Prayer, is in a sense a little vacation. A vacation is time out to practice just letting go and giving oneself over to the refreshing things of life. At least that is the theory. Sad to say, most people make such a project out of a vacation and try to cram so much into it and are so concerned about getting everything they can out of it that it is anything but refreshing—a time of letting go. But the theory is that it is a time of more intense practice in letting go and receiving, so that we can carry this back to the work world and work leisurely.

As I have said, leisure is found in balance—the ability to give and take in harmony even while we work. We give ourselves to the task, the work in hand, the realities involved, and let them speak to us. Then we take them in hand, and in harmony with their true nature and inner energies we do with them what we want to do. There is a constant listening in leisurely work. We are listening to all around us and all that is involved in our work, constantly letting it speak to us and impart to us its own inner strength, its own refreshing beauty and goodness.

The good carpenter listens with eye and hand and ear as he works his wood. He lets the wood speak to him. He goes with the grain, with the inbuilt movement and strengths of the wood. He allows the intrinsic beauty which nature has fashioned over the decades and maybe even centuries to come forth.

When we work with anything, this can be the case—above all when we work with people. This is the source of top-grade management. We learn to listen and allow the maximum potential of each person to come into play in our common task. We let our visions align themselves and then give direction to this powerful force.

Centering Prayer can be our twice-daily vacation, as we let go of any tensions that might have built up since our last "vacation." More important, it can school us in the art of giving ourselves in openness to the deepest sort of listening—worshipful, reverent listening to Reality in each person and each thing that comes into our lives and our labors. This is synonymous with constant prayer, for the worshipful listening is to that Reality who is our God. Giving ourselves to Reality this way is giving ourselves in love, love of God and love of all these expressions of his goodness, life, and love.

Another way of looking at these two balancing aspects of life is to consider the difference between purpose and meaning. When we take something or someone in hand we have a purpose: we want to do something with it, her, or him. We seek to attain an end, and when it is attained we are finished. No one keeps hammering a nail once it is in—or the job will be ruined. We might well be accused of playing around. We have switched over to meaning—opening ourselves to the meaning of a thing and just doing it for its own sake, for its inner meaning. We play for the sake of playing. We dance to dance. We gaze at a sunset just for the sake of its refreshing beauty. The time is not set by the completion of a task. We do it as long as we enjoy it, as long as it refreshes us. If it begins to tire us, we pass on.

If when we work for a purpose we also let the persons and things we are working with speak to us, we let their meaning in. Even as we are tired by our efforts we will be refreshed by the experience of Reality. Purpose and meaning will balance each other. There will be give-and-take. Our work will be leisurely. Our whole lives will be leisurely.

This openness to meaning is one of the reasons why people

who Center regularly seem to have such boundless energy. They are constantly refreshed even in the midst of their labors. This enables them to cut back on their sleep and other recreative activities, so they have more time for productive work. The investment of Centering Prayer is amply paid back. Anyone who says he or she has not the time to Center should perhaps take another look. If they are so hard-pressed they are perhaps the ones who most need Centering Prayer, not only to gain time and energy but to find leisure and worship and God in the midst of all their labors.

While speaking of labor I do want to add a word here about the Sabbath rest. Just because we have learned how to labor leisurely and therefore do not need to stop our labor for rest, this does not mean we should not still partake of this weekly day of holy rest. God certainly was in no way fatigued by the divine labors in the creation. And yet on the seventh day God rested.

The first sin was a sin of taking. Biblically, Eve reached out and took an apple. What she was trying to do was to take life, possess it of herself, be her own center. God had labored lovingly through six days and presented man with the gift of the creation. It was all gift. We know a gift is appreciated when it is used appropriately. But Adam and Eve did not appreciate the giftedness of it all. They resented the restraints of proper use. They wanted to be the masters of the gift as though it came from them rather than from the Other. The result was that they were cast out. The gift could not of its very nature any longer be gift to them, for they refused to receive it as gift.

Night came on the seventh day. It was for the two a terrifying night. Was it to be an endless, eternal night? At last the eighth day dawned, the first day of a new hope. The first and eighth of days. The Source of that hope in the fullness of time descended to this earth and into the line of Adam and Eve and undertook a labor of love. Finally, the Lord rested on the seventh day in the tomb near Calvary. Again, on the first and eighth of days a new hope broke forth out of the tomb—a hope that goes beyond the death that Adam's race has ceaselessly experienced.

No wonder then that those who have fully received the gift of creation and recreation have changed the day of rest from the seventh day of offense and entombment to the first and eighth of days, to the day of hope.

And we need that day of hope, the hope that lies in the fallow field of the jubilee year. The hope that says that all does not depend on our productiveness and labor; that ultimately it is all gift and we can rest in the gift. We need to waste our daily minutes in Centering Prayer. We need this more ample space to get in touch with our own native fallowness and to realize that all our fruitfulness is gift.

The new Sabbath should be a day of centeredness. A day when we lay aside as much as possible all peripheral cares and concerns and center upon the Center of all. And know the giftedness of all. It should be a day of profound refreshment, a day on which we learn how to receive and not take. A day on which we do not have to labor for life but receive it whole as gift.

Obviously the day invites us to spend more time in Centering Prayer. The day of rest invites us to rest ever more deeply in the Center. It invites us to give ourselves over as gift in all our giftedness.

In Centering Prayer we give ourselves directly, immediately, and freely to God in the Prayer. And God immediately gives us to all others in loving, caring service. This in its fullness includes another kind of giving—one that is essentially Christian because it is so Christlike and it fulfills preeminently one of Christ's commands.

Perhaps one of the most difficult commands that our Lord has given us is this: Love your enemies. But the Lord has pushed it even further. He requires us to forgive our enemies, for he has us constantly praying to the Father: "Forgive us our trespasses as we forgive those who have trespassed against us."

Forgiving is more than giving. It is a giving of ourselves to the other in such a way that we take upon ourselves the guilt he or she has incurred in offending us. Jesus is the supreme exemplar of this. He, our God, took upon himself all the guilt of all our sin so that he could totally forgive us, giving himself to us in a fullness of union beyond our comprehension.

When someone has done violence to us or treated us unjustly, there is true offense. We have received offense and not just taken offense, as we might do if we are not truly Centered. When we take offense the fault is ours and we have to let go of it and forgive ourselves. But when we have received offense there is guilt, and that guilt rests on those who have offended us. There is no way in which we can fully forgive our offenders and leave them under the burden of guilt. We must relieve them of that burden, and we can do that only by taking on the guilt ourselves. This is why it is so difficult to really forgive.

In the compassion flowing from the experience of solidarity that we have when we are in the Center, we already know that the guilt of our brother or sister is indeed ours to bear with him or her. Centering Prayer opens the space for true forgiveness. It does more. It makes it an almost automatic reality once we experience the Center.

The guilt does not in the end rest with us. In the experience of Christ in God, we know how totally the Lamb of God has taken away the sin of the world. Our personal guilt and all the possible guilt that we can take upon ourselves has been taken from our shoulders by one stronger than we, a Man strong with the strength of God who yet entered into all our weakness in order to express his compassion for us.

I do not think I need to elaborate how refreshing is the gift of total forgiveness, both given and received.

From the Center he says to us: "Come to me all you who labor and are heavily burdened and I will refresh you"—on every level of our being.

Where's the Cross?

If Centering Prayer is so refreshing and, indeed, refreshes one's entire life with those wonderful fruits of the Spirit: love, joy, peace, patience, benignity—oh, yes, and long-suffering—well, where is the suffering, where is the cross? Our Master has said: "If you would be my disciple you must take up your cross daily"—not weekly or monthly, but daily. The cross must be a daily part of Christian life. Well, where is it in a Centered life?

First of all, part of our daily cross may lie in making time for our Centering Prayer. All of us can live very full lives. God in his generosity has given each of us tremendous potential—though some, unfortunately, do not seem to recognize the immense possibilities their lives offer. Then he surrounds us with a multitude of brothers and sisters with whom we can share the adventures of life. There is so much to do, so many wonderful people to share with, we have to make choices. To make time for our Centering Prayer, we have to make the choice for God. We have to give some of our precious time, which is something of the very substance of our life. The choice usually means giving up some other good thing that we could be doing with that time. And not necessarily things for ourselves, but some of the good things we could be doing for others. That is often more difficult than giving up our own pleasures. There is a real choice here and a real sacrifice—especially when we do not feel like Centering or when the Prayer seems to be leading us only into darkness and desert, into the cloud of unknowing. Fidelity to practice can be a real walking with Christ, a faithful carrying of the daily cross.

Within the Prayer itself there is a constant choice to be made. Again and again we become aware of things, of others, of our doings, of ourselves. Each time we must choose to let go—or rather choose God—to return to the Presence and thus to let go of others, of our doings, and of our very self. We usually like to stay with our own thoughts, be they good or bad ones. After all they are our thoughts. But fidelity to the practice calls for letting them go and choosing God. This involves something of the detachment of the cross, of dying to self in order to live to God. Fidelity to the Prayer leads to a complete death for the false self—and no one likes to die, even when we know it is a false self that is dying, even when we know by faith that such a death opens out to a fuller and more wonderful life.

The aim of Centering is not to find twenty minutes of bliss twice a day. It is not to find some sort of escape that we might use more and more. This return to the Center, this embrace of God is the sourcing of life, the transformation of life, the birth of compassion leading to another whole way of living.

The choices we make in Centering Prayer follow through into life. The option for God before all else or in all else becomes the force of our life. Our prayer word or love word is a great help as we move into this. The word attains something of its own power to bring us to the Center into the Presence. Instead of staying in our useless thoughts, good, bad, or indifferent, when we become aware of their uselessness we move for a moment to the Center with our word and let them glide away. Instead of nurturing feelings and thoughts that are not life-giving, whether they be negative in regard to ourselves or in regard to others, we use our word to slip into the Presence and let the feelings and thoughts fade away. Instead of struggling with temptations, which only acknowledges their existence, reinforcing them and strengthening them, we ignore them—which most effectively robs them of their existence—as we turn with our word to the Center. All of this, of course, involves a constant dying to self, the superficial, inquisitive, managing, pleasure-seeking self. It becomes part of the cross that marks our day from end to end.

There is yet more. As we come to know by experience of the Center our oneness with each and every person, and also the potential goodness and happiness that is available to fill the life of each, we enter more and more into the compassion of Christ which is at the heart of his Passion. We love more deeply and more universally. We see more exquisitely how people cause themselves to suffer because they do not know their own beauty and lovableness, God's immense love for them, and the meaning of their lives.

In the face of this growing sensitivity to the needs of others and our own growing love and desire to help them, we suffer more and more from the reality of our own limitations. We seem to have so little time to help, such a short supply of energy, so few of the talents and abilities that are needed. If only we could do so much more, respond to so many more needs. We have to make painful but very real choices. We have to turn away and leave tremendous spiritual and material needs unmet, trusting in the mercy of God. I have already shared how being in touch with the divine creative Love present at the Center of our being we can in some way respond to all the hurt around us. Yet we still feel the anguish of walking down a street in Calcutta or through a slum in Haiti or through a refugee camp in Somalia or on the pathways of our hearts and know that many of those on whom we rest our eyes or whom we touch with our hands, no matter how great our anguish and our desire to help, will yet starve to death or survive only in a very truncated human existence. Who will preach to them to give them the food of hope? Who will teach them to give them the opportunity to use their God-given talents? Who will clothe them so that they can preserve their human dignity? (One of the vivid memories I have of the slums of Haiti is of twelve-year-old boys going about naked because they need to save their one pair of shorts so they can appear in class. It is a crucial time in life for a young man to be so exposed.) Who will feed them so that they may preserve their very existence on this earth?

Fidelity to Centering Prayer will not only bring us a deepening joy but also a deepening share in all the suffering of our human race, of our desecrated earth. For we come to love the earth, too—the footstool of God. Ecological violence is a desecration in itself and a blatant ingratitude, even before it begins to threaten the life and well-being of the citizens of the earth, the children of God. The unhealed gash of strip mining, the polluted smog that dims the eyes of sun and moon, the acid rain that takes the healing out of nature's tears, the radiation that turns the life force of breath into death—all of these many wounds pierce the Centered one who knows he or she is one with the earth. They become a sharing in the wounds of Christ, as naked as were his wounds when he hung upon the cross. And what can we do? How helpless we feel as we hold the wounded and dying earth in a creative love that is rejected!

This is perhaps where our participation in the cross becomes most keen: when there is something we can do, yet we are not allowed to do it; when people will not let us into their lives with what we have to give—at least our love and care and support. There are not many places in the Scriptures where we read that God wept. He was often enough kind and compassionate and loving and even angry and punishing but rarely are we told that he wept. The Lord wept at death, his own death and the death of a friend. In both these cases his tears bore fruit in renewed life. But in one place his tears are the burning tears of utter frustration. He climbed the hill overlooking Jerusalem and using tender, motherly imagery he bewailed the fact that a wounded people would not let him heal them, an enslaved people would not let him liberate them. Jesus wept over Jerusalem and we weep with him every time we see the doors close before our—his, yours, and mine—healing love.

Where is the cross in a Centered life? It is where Jesus found it because we have become more like him, our true selves, Christed in baptism. With him we weep, intercede, and offer up the splinters and beams of the cross that the Father allows to be placed on our shoulders or invites us to carry with the Christ in others, as did Simon of Cyrene.

Centering Prayer does not take the cross out of life. But it opens us to experience one of the incomprehensible elements of the mystery of the cross.

Jesus' suffering on the cross reached the apex of human suffering. His absolutely exquisite body experienced the violence heaped upon it as fully as would ever be possible. His refined sensitivity knew to the depths the indignities and barbarism that were poured out upon him. The sense of sin and rejection crushed the very soul of this man who truly knew the Father and knew what sin is and yet took upon himself every sin—my sin and your sin and the ocean of sin around us, and through all the ages. Never has human suffering been so complete.

Yet this person is the very Son of God, one with the Father in the glory that was his from before time. At no moment was his beatitude diminished. The depths of suffering and the heights of glory hung together on the cross.

Theologians have pondered again and again this mystery. Using the rational mind, faith has sought understanding. And again and again they have fallen on one side or the other of the mystery.

But in Centering Prayer we are brought into the experience of this mystery of the cross and allowed to share in it. This happens when we come to know in the depths of our being the presence and love of God which fills us with abiding and abounding joy, even while compassion brings into us an ever fuller share in the sufferings of the human family and of all the earth.

Here is the cross in Centering Prayer: arms stretching out horizontally to embrace the whole of the cosmos in all its groanings, a life deeply planted in the Center of the earth and yet in the very Center of heaven, in the Center of God, a life reaching vertically up into the very heights of divine Life and Love and Being.

Has the Lord Gone
to Dalmanutha?

Saint Mark opens the eighth chapter of his Gospel with the well-known story of the multiplication of the loaves and fishes:

And now once again a great crowd had gathered and they had nothing to eat. So Jesus called his disciples to him and said to them, "I feel sorry for all these people; they have been with me for three days and have nothing to eat. If I send them off hungry they will collapse on the way; some have come a great distance." His disciples replied: "Where could anyone get bread to feed these people in a deserted place like this?" Jesus asked them: "How many loaves do you have?" "Seven," they said. Then he instructed the crowd to sit down on the ground and he took the seven loaves. After giving thanks, he broke them and gave them to his disciples to distribute and they distributed them among the crowd. They had a few small fish as well and over these he said a blessing and ordered them to be distributed as well. All ate as much as they wanted and then collected seven basketfuls of scraps. There were about four thousand in the crowd. Jesus sent them on their way and getting into a boat with his disciples he went to Dalmanutha.

When we begin to abide with the Lord in the Center, usually after a relatively short time—"they have been with me for three days"—and sometimes immediately, the Lord begins to feed us in his own wonderful way. This is true even for those who "have come a great distance"—those who have come into Centering Prayer from a life that had been marked not by prayer but rather by indifference or even sin. The Lord is good. He takes the little we bring, be it but seven loaves and a few small fish—the seven gifts of the Spirit given to us at baptism and the few virtues we have managed to catch ourselves over the years—and uses them to richly feed us. And not only us, but all who are with us, all those we carry with us in our hearts. He feeds us superabundantly. As we come forth from the Center the seven gifts become sources of abundant food for our ongoing life and for all those we can serve.

And all the Lord has asked of us is that we "sit down on the ground"; that is, that we sit down humbly and prepare ourselves to receive and enjoy, to eat our fill. That is all that Centering Prayer is—sitting down humbly and hungry and willing to receive.

We want more of this food. We return again and again. Perhaps we do not sense we have gotten our fill or that we have those basketfuls to bring back to everyday life. Fortunate are we if the Lord continues to be there for us, filling us again and again.

But sooner or later it will probably be our experience that the Lord has sailed for Dalmanutha. He has shipped out. All we find when we return to the Center is an apparently "deserted place." People sometimes speak of this experience, quite aptly, as "dryness" or aridity. There seems to be nothing to nourish us now, and no one there. The Lord seems to have left us. Why is this?

Well, as we have said, sometimes our experience is clearly that the Lord has not yet filled us. Sometimes he seems to have filled us and even given us a supply for life, but it seems to disappear all too quickly. The Lord cannot totally fill us and fill us in such a way that we become a veritable source, even as he is source—"Out of him will flow rivers of living water"—until we open all the corners of our being to him, until we truly hunger for him, having left behind all other food. So one of the reasons why the Lord takes off for Dalmanutha is so that our hunger for him may increase. Having tasted, we will hunger yet more. We will use up all the crumbs of earthly satisfaction by which we have heretofore been nourished and seek only the food that he alone can give. We are left high and dry so that we will thirst all the more for the living water. We are left in the shadow of a cloud of unknowing so that we will push our way all the more eagerly through it toward the Sun, leaving all earthly cares behind in a cloud of forgetfulness.

We know from the Gospel of Saint John that the crowd for the most part did not remain in the desert. They went in pursuit of the Lord in a reasonable way. They wanted explanations.

The Lord was good enough to respond to them. He told those would-be disciples who were not willing to remain in the desert, in the dryness, that what they in fact were seeking was only the passing satisfaction. They liked the sweet taste, the sense of fullness, something for nothing. What he wanted to give them was so much more. Beyond morsels of consolation and satisfaction or a feeling of fullness, he wanted to give them that food which would transform them and divinize them and truly nourish his divine life and being in them. This was too much for them. They walked no more with him.

So, too, it often happens. We first dare to go to the inner place, to the Center, because, though we perceive it as a deserted place, we are led by him and in some way encouraged by others. Perhaps we are even accompanied by others in a workshop or a retreat. The Lord soon begins to feed us, but it is in good part a bread of this world: some peace, some joy, some new clarity. It is good. It is his gift. It nourishes our pilgrim life.

Then he begins to play hide-and-seek with us. He does this first of all so that he can draw forth from us a greater hunger and lead us to a more dedicated seeking and a greater detachment from the things of the world. He opens ever greater spaces within our spirit, within our lives, so that he can fill us more and more with these good gifts, fill our lives more with his joy.

But he is not content with this. He wants to bring us further, to a transformation of consciousness, to unity-consciousness, to a full possession of our divinization. Even as he has filled us with his gifts, he must yet free us from them so that we will not seek them as the substance that will fill us but let them be the accidents which attend the supersubstantial banquet of his very self.

Centering Prayer is seeking God and nothing less than God. As the author of *The Cloud of Unknowing* says: "Let this little word represent to you God in all God's fullness and nothing less than the fullness of God. Let nothing but God hold sway in your mind and heart." It is to this purity of heart that the Lord would lead us.

When the Lord ships out to Dalmanutha, this is when many fall away. The "deserted place" within is experienced as dry and dark. Reason tries to lead us out, back to the level of everyday thought, where we can question and argue, and see clearly the irrationality of a human person eating divine food, becoming one with the Father in the Son, and living by the Spirit of God. We will not follow this Master into the place deserted of reason, the land of faith that opens out into new levels of consciousness, which human reason can only see as void. Why waste time in what seems to be only a "deserted place"?

Saint John tells us that when the crowds refused to give Jesus their faith and follow him into the new realms he was opening out to them, Jesus turned to the Twelve and asked what they were going to do. Peter spoke up. Peter, as human as any man, with as many faults and failures as the worst of us, this man who would in his day have his fall and even deny the Lord, spoke up here. It is a magnificent profession of faith: "Lord, to whom shall we go? You have the words of eternal life."

The Lord turns to you and to me, and he asks us, too: "Will you go away or will you abide with me?" Lord, to whom can we go? Is there any other hope open to us to find the fullness of life which we restlessly seek? "Our hearts are made for you, O Lord, and they will not rest until they rest in you." You have the words of eternal life. You are the way and the truth and the life. To whom shall we go? We can but return to the "deserted place," beneath the cloud of unknowing, and abide there. And lo, suddenly and soon enough, the cloud will part and in a new light that the Spirit enkindles within us we will perceive that it is not a deserted place but, indeed, the very Center of the cosmos, the very Center of God.

When we experience what is called dryness, let us not be too quick to judge that the Lord has gone to Dalmanutha. Let us first examine ourselves. Dryness, as it is called, comes from our not getting what we want. Usually it is experienced because we are still seeking the sweet waters of sensible consolations, good feelings, and rational insights—the things that satisfy our natural desires. If we can lay aside our desire for these things and seek only to be to God, giving ourselves to God in faith and love, opening the space for God to show up, we may well find the Lord has not gone to Dalmanutha at all. God has been with us all the time, but we have not perceived the Presence because we have been too busy seeking those other things. Indeed, if we constantly strive to seek God and God alone, as the author of *The Cloud* directs us, the Lord may never have to depart for Dalmanutha. God may just continue to feed us in a new way that will open out in us the gifts of understanding and wisdom and lead us directly into the experience of God in the purity of unity-consciousness.

We should be concerned about purifying our intent in prayer, striving to seek the God of consolations rather than the consolations of God. Doing that, we should not be too concerned about what goes on—whether the Lord does in fact leave for Dalmanutha or not. That is his business. Ours is to give ourselves to God as completely as we can in love. And then respect God's sovereign freedom to respond to us in any way God wills, totally trusting the infinite and all-compassionate Love to respond to us in the way that is truly best for us. "For those who love God, all things work together unto good." In the simplicity of such a faith and hope we can abide peacefully and joyfully even in an apparently "deserted place," in a cloud of unknowing. If the Lord seems to have sailed for Dalmanutha, let us be confident that the Holy One will return soon enough. In fact, God is not gone from us. For when we are at the Center, we are at the Center of all, even at the Center of Dalmanutha.

Sharing
the Gift

Freely have you received, freely give." These words of the Lord to us flow directly from the second great commandment, which is like unto the first: "Love your neighbor as you love yourself." If we have found in Centering Prayer something that is good, that has enriched and renewed our lives, then in love we should want our neighbor to share in this blessing.

Although it is quite natural for us to want to share with others when we find something that is good, there are at the same time certain things that hold us back—especially when that good is of the spiritual order. We need to look at this a bit. We also need to look at what we must have in order to be able to share the Prayer effectively with others. Very frequently I find exaggerated ideas in this area. There are also inhibitions and questions about sharing this precious gift—with whom can we share it?

We will look at these questions. Then we will look at the actual sharing and the necessary follow-up, as well as the formation of Centering Prayer groups.

Finally, we will look at this gift in relation to other religious traditions.

Necessarily, this part of the book is rather pragmatic but I hope some real wisdom is seeded within it.

> You must proclaim what God has done for you.
> God has called you out of darkness
> into God's own wonderful light.
> *(1 Peter 2:9)*

Courage!

There is a natural instinct in us to want to share with others when we have found something good. Remember the little story Jesus told of the woman who lost one of her silver pieces: she scoured the house, and when she found it she called in all her neighbors and invited them to rejoice with her.

That may be a good way to do it—to share the Prayer. When we have found our Center, something most precious that we have lost through no fault of our own, we might well invite in the neighbors and share our find with them. Invite them on a journey to self-discovery, invite them to discover the wonder and love of their God.

I suspect as you were reading the previous paragraph more than one reservation—if not sheer panic—popped into your head at the thought of gathering your particular neighbors in your living room and leading them into Centering Prayer. Why?

Something in our American culture looms up here. The exaggerated insistence, especially in modern times, on separation between church and state has relegated the former to being something very private. Among many Americans it is considered almost gauche to bring up the subject of religion, except perhaps in a most abstract way. To talk about one's own religious experience—well, those fundamentalists do that in their churches, and sometimes outside. But that is their way. Most well-mannered Americans do not speak about their own religious activity lest they seem to be proselytizing or trying to force something on others. We must not intrude on another's privacy and religious freedom.

Certainly it is very important to fully respect the freedom of others. In a matter so personal and deep and important as one's religious practice, a certain delicacy is called for. But religion is not wholly a private affair. There is social responsibility and social sin. We all have a responsibility to see that our country fulfills its God-given roles and responsibilities among the family of nations and in regard to our fellow citizens. I do not think anyone will deny that we need to heighten our moral consciousness as a nation in both regards. There is probably no way to raise consciousness more effectively, with the highest respect for the individual, than to help others find their own true self in God. With delicacy and with a generous and courageous heart, we can gently offer this Centering Prayer to others as gift.

We Catholics, though, have another widespread hang-up—a diminishing one, I am happy to say. That is our clericalism. It is for the priest and the religious to speak about religious things, to teach prayer—not a humble lay person. The charismatic renewal brought about a wonderful breakthrough in this area. In the power of the Spirit, often reinforced by strong emotions, lay persons did begin to bring others into deep personal prayer and lead prayer groups and give teachings. They even reached out and tried to minister to priests and religious.

There have been many happy breakthroughs in regard to teaching Centering Prayer on the part of both lay persons and religious women. I have already spoken in this book about some of these lay teachers. Here is a letter I recently received from a sister:

> I never felt that this was something I had gifts for. But last week, when it became clear that it was going to be difficult for Father to preach on Sunday, for a variety of reasons, I found myself considering the possibility. I had looked at the readings and found that they spoke to me and were expressive of the experience of last week's class. So, thinking about what you had said about having "courage," I offered to do the homily. It

went well. Amazingly, I actually enjoyed doing it…after the great nervousness of the immediate anticipation. People were listening very attentively and I got positive responses after the Masses. Many people took the article "The Centering Prayer" that I made available. Thank you for your sharings and encouragements. I have "discovered" Centering Prayer, enjoy it, and look forward to other opportunities to share it with others.

The nervousness or fear of which Sister speaks is a very real thing. You can imagine how much fear a young priest or a deacon has the first time he ascends a pulpit. I still experience some nervousness every time I step before an unknown audience or even with a known audience when I am going to share something very personal. It certainly leaves one exposed. But I think a little fear or nervousness is good. It tones up our delivery.

There can be, of course, some objective fear about our competence. In our next chapter we will talk about what we need to share Centering Prayer. But even when we know our stuff, so to speak, there is the fear of not being able to put it across right for this particular audience. Here we need to trust in Holy Spirit. It is very clear to me that nothing I ever say or do will have any effect if the Spirit does not work within the person. At the same time, she can use my poor sputterings to accomplish her ends. Didn't she use Balaam's ass? So she certainly can use this one, too.

When I was a young priest I received a real gift from the Lord in this regard. At that time a very famous preacher visited the abbey. He was rated second only to the then Monsignor Sheen. In the course of his talk to us, he shared the following incident from his early priesthood. He was already packing them in and having great results. One day, after he had spoken before a packed church, a very old man came into the sacristy and asked to go to confession. The old man told the priest he had not been to the sacraments in over sixty years. This particular day, a very cold winter's day, he had stepped into the church just to find a little warmth before continuing on his way. Father was in the pulpit and the old man began to listen. Something Father said touched his heart and he had to come back to the Lord. The priest told us he then succumbed to a movement of pride and impulsively asked the old man what it was that had so moved him. Father almost fell out of the confessional when the old fellow replied: "It was when you said, 'I'll tell it to the Little Flower.'" Father could not remember having said that or having any intention to say such a thing. Indeed, he was not sure whether it was supposed to refer to Saint Thérèse of Lisieux or the then mayor of New York who enjoyed the same nickname. What he did know was the unforgettable lesson that it was not what he said or how he said it but how God enabled people to hear that made the difference.

We offer what we can. Results are God's business.

Yet there is in us a fear of rejection. People might not respond—and we hate to waste time—or they might clearly reject what we offer. Was this not the fate of our Master? It was one of the things that brought him to tears. And he foretold that his disciples would meet a like fate. Of course, we will never experience rejection if we never make any attempt to share. But if we do attempt, and we are rejected, we have the joy and consolation of knowing that the experience makes us more Christlike.

If people do not seem to respond immediately to our sharing it might be well for us to remember those words of the apostle Paul: "One sows, another waters, and God gives the increase." We may be sowing—for this person, within whom the seed will rest until watered by another; or for the one to whom this person will pass on the seed. It is going to be delightfully interesting in heaven to see what God did do with all the seeds we have scattered.

We may be watering. It yet remains for the Lord to give the increase when and how he wishes. He knows what is best for our friends. That is what we want for them. We can trust him.

There is a command in the gospels: "Be perfect, even as

your heavenly Father is perfect." It is a rather frightening command if taken out of its context. The Lord goes on to say: "He allows his rain to fall on the just and the unjust alike." Our perfection lies in our universal love. We are to love everyone and share what we have with all. But like God we have to respect totally the freedom of each. God constantly pours out the rain of divine grace on us all and each is completely free to accept the gift or refuse it.

Freely have we received. Like our heavenly Father, let us freely share. But let our sharing be as gentle as a springtime rain and given with much space for the recipients to take and receive as fully and as freely as they wish. Let us have the courage, at least in this little way, to lay down our lives for our friends.

Sharers of the Word

A mong the joys and consolations the Lord gives me are the many letters that come from all parts of the world in which wonderful people share what Centering Prayer has meant to them and how they are sharing it with others. Here is one that recently came from the Philippines:

I have before me your book on *Centering Prayer—Renewing an Ancient Christian Prayer Form*. This book was God-sent and was literally placed in my hands by Holy Spirit. Almost a year ago in July 1984, I was undergoing what my spiritual confessor called "a desert experience." In desperation, one afternoon, I asked my daughter to drop me at a bookstore before going to class. I thought I might divert my attention from the wretched feeling I had. As I browsed around the books, I was continually praying to Holy Spirit to guide me to a book that would help me get out of the misery I was in. Time passed so quickly I panicked when I heard my daughter tooting the horn of her car. I couldn't go home empty-handed so I grabbed the book closest to me and paid for it. It took some time before I could get myself to read the book—I was in such a state that I could not find consolation in anything....I was fearful of praying (it filled me with fear and apprehension), Mass was simply something to pass the time, books couldn't hold my attention for any length of time (they were simply words). However I persevered with my prayers, going to Mass daily and trying to read. Slowly your book on Centering Prayer started to make sense. I found I could pray without being apprehensive (as I prayed to be lifted out of my misery, the dwelling on my misery made me fearful of prayer—a vicious cycle had taken place) and, for the duration of my Centering, I had forgotten self and focused my attention on God....I have been talking of Centering Prayer to anyone who gives me five minutes of his/her time. I am slowly but surely introducing Centering Prayer to our parish here in the Philippines. Our pastor has gathered a group (his counselees) and they want to experience Centering Prayer (him included). I have set this for after Pentecost. Being a formator of our Secular Franciscan Order, I have introduced Centering Prayer to our novices who now meet every week for Bible sharing and Centering Prayer. Other groups outside my parish have also heard of Centering Prayer and have asked me to talk to them about it. That Centering Prayer has transformed me is a gross understatement. I have done things I never imagined I could do. I could never talk before a crowd. I would not even venture to lead the rosary unless I had the prayers before me because I would get so nervous I would forget the Our Father (which has happened several times). Now I still die a thousand times while talking before a group of people but somehow I seem to get the courage to do it in my desire to bring Centering Prayer to my friends. What Centering Prayer has done for me is something I cannot put into words...it has brought God, Our Father, Jesus, Our Brother, in union with Holy Spirit, to me. The reality of this is beyond words.

Our parish is quite unique in the sense that of the 5 percent of Filipino's who form the top of the economic bracket, 3 percent are parishioners here...the "cream of the crop" economically and intellectually but strugglers spiritually.

This woman's experience challenges us to reflect on just what is necessary for one to be an effective teacher of Centering Prayer. What are the qualities needed?

I would say knowledge, some personal experience, faith, courage, love, and compassion.

How much does one need to *know?* Actually, very little. Just the essentials of the practice. We will talk about what these are after the next chapter. To be able to simply and clearly share the Three Rules or Guidelines is enough. But it is important to be able to share them out of personal experience, however little. Our knowledge should be experiential. Then we share what we have done.

I have spoken before of the experience of one middle-aged sister. In the final session of every retreat or workshop I encourage all the participants to go out and share what they have received. They have had enough experience in the course of their time together to teach or share out of their experience. This little sister told me later that as she left she shook her head and thought: Well, maybe someday I will be ready, but it will be quite a while. That evening she returned home to the apartment she shared with three other sisters. They were full of curiosity about her workshop. Before she knew it the four of them were sitting in the Silence of Centering Prayer. The next morning during the coffee break at the motherhouse, again the curiosity was strong and Sister shared—and soon all were Centering. They agreed to meet at four-thirty in the lounge for another session together. By the end of the week ninety sisters were Centering together in the lounge at four-thirty, having made a commitment to Center on their own in the morning before coming to work. When Sister met me, they were making plans to bring Centering Prayer to the whole congregation. Yes, it would be "quite a while" before Sister was ready to share—about four hours, or as long as it took her to get home!

My correspondent from the Philippines did not have the advantage of a workshop or the experience of Centering with others. She had to start on her own in a time of struggle with only the book. But that was enough. Centering Prayer is so simple—anyone can teach it, even after very little experience. It is good to be a learner walking with learners. After all, in this matter of prayer we are all always learners. "We do not know how to pray as we ought, but Holy Spirit teaches us."

That is one of the reasons why *faith* is so important in one who will share with others. We have to rely on Holy Spirit to teach from within even as we speak without. That is why it is supremely important *always* to enter into the Prayer with those with whom we are sharing and give the Spirit a chance to do some teaching.

Faith is essential because it is impossible to pray or experience the Prayer without faith. Centering Prayer is not just a technique. It is being to God in faith and love. If we do not have faith and reach out to the hidden God in that faith-filled love, we are just going through the movements. Perhaps we are finding a little natural peace and quiet but little more.

With living faith, we can trust that Holy Spirit will back us up. This gives us the *courage* to step out. We know we cannot actually "teach" prayer. We can only show others how to open the space so that Holy Spirit can teach them. We can count on the Spirit to back us up.

One of the things we fear is that the person(s) with whom we are sharing the Prayer will ask questions we cannot answer. Oftentimes we will discover that Holy Spirit gives us the answers they need. This is one reason why I very much appreciate any opportunity to share with others: they ask questions I have never thought of before, and I find myself giving answers which are as enlightening to me as to the questioner.

Actually, it is good when we simply cannot give an answer. (Sometimes the Spirit leaves us in our ignorance.) To have to say "I don't know, but I will find out" has two benefits. It impels us to do more study or return to our own teacher to learn yet more about the Prayer. It also assures the learner that it isn't necessary to have all the answers to use the Prayer fruitfully. That is very good. The open acceptance of our limitations in experience and knowledge will encourage the beginner.

The more you are an ordinary, everyday person, the more

encouraging you will be to others as a teacher of Centering Prayer. Remember Dan, about whom I spoke earlier in this book. Centering Prayer is the simple prayer of the people. In the Middle Ages it was taught by uneducated lay brothers working on the farms and sheep runs and in the fairs. It was the prayer of these humble, hardworking men that led to everyday contemplatives and saints.

Love is the important thing. First of all, the love of God. That is the whole essence of this Prayer, which is a simple and pure gift of self in love to God. And it is love for God that impels us to enter into God's desire for intimacy with each and every one and to do all we can for its fulfillment. "The love of Christ impels us."

It is our love for God and our love in God for our sisters and brothers that impels us to step out and go beyond ourselves in what we may experience as risky and vulnerable—to lay down our lives for the other, remembering our self-giving Master's command to love as he has loved.

That fullness of love that is *compassion* enables us to walk with our sisters and brothers in their first efforts and on through, as they seek the Lord within. Their experience might be very different from ours. They may be very faltering in their first steps and need a lot of time and encouragement. They might be demanding and bring out our ignorance in a way that is repeatedly humbling for us. Or, what can be more humbling, the Lord might run out to them like the Prodigal Father and heap blessings upon them, bringing them into a rich banquet, while we, the faithful ones, never even seem to get a decent sandwich. That God of ours—full of surprises. God just is not fair. God gives out the divine largess in whatever way it pleases the Three.

Compassion does not just mean being with another in his or her sufferings. The root is the Latin word *pati*; it means to experience any kind of emotion—good or bad. Compassion calls for us to rejoice with those who rejoice just as much as to weep with those who weep. A beginner who is having wonderful experiences of God's presence and love—perhaps after years of sin and neglect or years of lukewarmness or dryness—usually needs a lot of reassurance that this is OK. They have every right to enjoy the consolations of God just as long as they are seeking the God of consolations and not just consolations for themselves. For one who has never before had an experience of God and the divine love, this can seem to be far too good to be true. They need to be reassured it is true. God does love them with an overwhelming love. If a humble person has trudged along, perhaps for years, in quiet fidelity and is suddenly invaded by the Reality that he or she had thought was reserved for the great saints or for heaven, that person is going to need a great deal of compassionate encouragement. The Lord will do his part. But friends are a big help, especially the friend who opened up this space by talking about three simple rules or guidelines.

In a certain sense, then, a lot is expected of us if we are to be effective teachers. But it is not in the direction most of us usually think of: lots of knowledge and experience. It is in the direction in which we all do want to grow: in the direction of love and compassion. Yet this may be one of the things that does hold us back. We do not want to take on that burden of love and support. But what is Christian life about if it is not about growing in love—love of God and love of one another, which means support?

We do not need to be daunted by the fact that we know little or have never cast ourselves in the role of teacher. Simply sharing our personal experience—a beautiful gift of self—can open space for those with whom we share. It may reveal to them unknown possibilities and give birth to new hopes. When we do this—and it is the first and essential thing—they can, if need be, turn to others or to books and tapes to get more formal teaching. But don't be too quick to pass by the grace of teaching.

In reality, it is always the one who teaches who gets more out of the teaching than the one who is taught—for all that the learner receives passes through the teacher. And, more important, the teacher grows in love, self-giving love. It is something like our Lord's Passion. He died for us and for our salvation. But no one will ever obtain more glory from Calvary's hill than the Sacred Victim himself. Our most gracious God never invites us to do anything for others without it being in the divine design that we, the doers, will be the ones most to profit by it. What a wonderful God!

So, you know the Three Rules or Guidelines. Muster up your courage and in love go forth. Share the Prayer with all you meet. Welcome them into the Center, where you can love and enjoy them all the more—and where they can come to appreciate, love, and enjoy you all the more.

Return to the Father

All of us are, in our very being, a response to the creative Love of God which has called us into being and at every moment sustains us in that being. It is of our very nature to be a response to God's love. Yet our true nature is all too often overlaid by a false self, a false identity which cloaks our true nature and keeps us from true happiness. We sense this at times and experience a deep, urgent need to throw off the cloak, walk in the light, and discover ourselves. This need, as natural as it is, is the voice of God within us inviting us to come home to God, to come into God's light, to come to the Center. This need, experienced in different ways, leads many to seek Centering Prayer.

I am sure that our monastery is not the only place that has had the experience of young persons coming, knocking on the door, and asking: "Will you teach us how to meditate?" What do I do in a case like this? I sit our friends down and very briefly give them the Three Rules. With this modification: instead of having them choose a love word that is meaningful to them—which might be difficult or impossible for them to do—I give them as their word the holy Name, Jesus. Then we meditate together for twenty minutes.

They usually have a good experience. When the prodigal starts his or her journey home, the Father runs out in welcome. As a result, they know Jesus has something to do with what they are seeking and they have some confidence in me as a teacher. After answering any questions they pose, I advise them to continue practicing the meditation twice a day, for twenty minutes each time. Then I present them with a small

156

New Testament or a copy of the Gospel of Saint John. I try to impress on them that this is a very sacred book. They should guard it with great reverence and once a day listen to it for at least ten minutes. (They will usually read the whole book from cover to cover immediately but then take up the prescribed practice of daily listening.) "Faith comes through hearing." With the listening and the Centering, the Prodigal Father runs out and embraces the child who has been enticed—unknown God though this might be to them in their first searching steps.

I have alluded to the prodigal several times in this book. In truth, we are all prodigals in one way or another. Let us listen again to this wonderful gospel story. It is always fun to hear old favorites.

A man had two sons. The younger said to his father: "Father, let me have the share of the estate that would come to me." So the father divided the property between them. A few days later the younger got together everything he had and left for a distant country where he squandered his money on a life of debauchery.

When he had spent it all that country experienced a severe famine. Now he began to feel the pinch so he hired himself out to one of the local inhabitants who put him on his farm to feed the pigs. The son would have willingly filled his belly with the husks the pigs were eating but no one offered him anything. Then he came to himself and said: "How many of my father's paid servants have more food than they want and here I am dying of hunger. I will leave this place and go to my father and say: 'Father, I have sinned against heaven and against you; I no longer deserve to be called your son; treat me as one of your paid servants.'" So he left the place and went back to his father.

While he was still a long way off, his father saw him and was moved with pity. He ran to the boy, clasped him in his arms and kissed him tenderly. Then his son said: "Father, I have sinned against heaven and

against you. I no longer deserve to be called your son."
But the father said to his servants: "Quick. Bring out
the best robe and put it upon him. Put a ring on his
finger and sandals on his feet. Bring the calf we have
been fattening and kill it; we are going to have a feast,
a celebration, because this son of mine was dead and
has come back to life, he was lost and is found." And
they began to celebrate.

Now the elder son was out in the fields. On his
way back, as he drew near the house, he could hear
music and dancing. Calling one of the servants, he
asked what was going on. "Your brother has come,"
replied the servant, "and your father has killed the calf
we have fattened because he has got him back safe
and sound." He was angry and refused to go in. His
father came out to plead with him; but he answered
his father: "Look, all these years I have slaved for you
and never once disobeyed your orders, yet you never
gave me so much as a kid to celebrate with my friends.
But for this son of yours, when he comes back after
swallowing up your property—he and his women—
you kill the calf we have been fattening."

The father said: "My son, you are with me always
and all that I have is yours. But it was only right we
should celebrate and rejoice, because your brother here
was dead and has come to life; he was lost and is found"
(Luke 15:11–32).

There is an obvious meaning to this parable: the prodigal is
the one who seeks his happiness in the false pleasures of the
world. (The young people who come to our door are often
such.) The prodigal "comes to himself" when he realizes that
he is still a son, that in spite of everything he still has a Father
to whom he can turn.

But for those of us who have never apparently left the
household of the Father there is another, more subtle, way in
which we sometimes squander the riches of our inheritance

and go into the foreign land, the region of unlikeness. The danger for us, who have the knowledge of the faith, is that we may forget that in truth we are always seeking a hidden and truly unknown God. We can fool ourselves into thinking that our poor concepts and images really do portray God to us. With our many thoughts and images we can act like the prodigal son. We can take our rich heritage as the children of God and go into a land of unlikeness where we create a God like unto ourselves. We then revel in the pseudo-richness of our religious concepts and images. Soon enough they fail to satisfy us. We begin to hunger. We want to find the kind of satisfaction that animals find in their experience of things at their own proper level. We, too, have been made to experience— but to experience something that is infinitely beyond this creation. In the realization of this, we prodigals "come to ourselves."

Whatever may be our form of prodigality, Centering Prayer can be for us the process of coming to ourselves. We come to perceive how we have betrayed ourselves. We resolve to leave the land of the unlikeness and return to the true Center, where we can live according to our true nature, that of children of the Father, albeit unworthy. As soon as we begin to act on this resolve, the watchful and waiting Father, who has been ever present with his grace, reaches out and embraces us and begins to bestow on us the fruits of the Spirit. We can enter into the joys of the household as our very own, even though we know they are undeserved gifts.

To begin Centering Prayer, all that is needed is some sort of desire to return to the Center, to return to God, however implicit. This may be induced by our experience of the Revelation or by any other means. God can and does work in and through all things, drawing us. As we begin to respond and practice the Prayer, it will become more and more evident that "being with God in faith and love" demands that we build up our faith and purify our hearts. Anything we are doing that is contrary to God's will must be left behind if we are to continue in the way of the Prayer. This realization grows with the practice. But to begin the journey to the Center, to begin Centering Prayer, the least bit of faith—even apparently human faith—that God can be sought within and the desire to do this are enough to begin the Prayer. The prodigal has but to turn from false gods and he or she can start down the road to the Center.

Some of the statements made by the author of *The Cloud of Unknowing* seem to indicate that this wise old spiritual father would be more restrictive in regards to sharing the Prayer. We must keep in mind in reading him that he is writing in a totally Catholic milieu. He expects that all his possible readers will be members of the Catholic Church, with the responsibilities of one educated in at least the rudiments of the Faith. As a spiritual father, he does not want to be responsible for leading anyone into some sort of pseudo-mysticism or false contemplation. The demands he makes in the foreword of his book, reiterated elsewhere in his treatise, do seem rather highly set: "I have in mind a person who, over and above the good works of the active life, has resolved to follow Christ (as far as is humanly possible with God's grace) into the inmost depths of contemplation [or, as we have expressed it, into the Center] ...who has first been faithful for some time to the demands of the active life...."

When the Father, in the body of the book, comes to express concretely what this means, he is not as demanding as we might have expected: "If you ask me when a person should begin the contemplative work I would answer: not until he has first purified his conscience of all particular sins in the Sacrament of Penance as the Church prescribes...once having done what the Church requires, he should fearlessly begin the contemplative work" (Chapter 28). So the requirement to be "faithful for some time to the demands of the active life" is indeed minimal. The Father simply asks for a conversion, a turning back to God, expressed in what is the required way for Catholics. For the Father it matters little if one has been a prodigal—"some who have been hardened, habitual sinners arrive at the perfection of this work sooner than those who have never sinned grievously" (Chapter 29); or if one is beset with present weakness—"In choosing your present way of life you made a radical commitment to God and this remains despite temporary lapses" (Chapter 10). (The Father seems decidedly up-to-date in speaking here about a "fundamental option.") The only thing that matters is one's true desire: "It is not what you are nor what you have been that God sees with his all-merciful eyes, but what you desire to be" (Chapter 75). Going on to close the treatise with a quote from Saint Augustine—"The entire life of a good Christian is nothing less than holy desire"—the Father seems clearly to indicate this way of contemplative prayer is for all Christians. However, he always retains a deep respect for the diverse ways in which God leads us. This theme is well developed by the Father, with biblical imagery, in several chapters (71–73). Here he says: "It is important to realize that in the interior life we must never take our own experiences (or lack of them) as the norm for everyone else." Earlier he was affirmed: "How often it happens that the grace of contemplation will awaken in people of every walk and station of life... religious and lay alike" (Chapter 18).

Far from excluding anyone from the attempt to develop the contemplative dimension of life, the Father seems to imply that its development is essential for the fulfillment of human life: "It is God, and he alone, who can fully satisfy the hunger and longing of our spirit which, transformed by his redeeming grace, is enabled to embrace him by love" (Chapter 4). "The activities of the lower degree of the active life [the corporal works of mercy] in themselves leave much of man's natural human potential untapped. At this stage he lives, as it were, outside himself and beneath himself. As he advances to the higher degree of the active life (which merges with the lower degree of the contemplative life) he becomes increasingly interior, living more from the depths of himself and becoming, therefore, more fully human" (Chapter 8).

Since the author of *The Cloud of Unknowing* is writing for Christians in a wholly Catholic context, his teaching has to be adapted in its application to others. The same honesty and sincerity in one's desire for God—as God is perceived—are necessary but the way this is expressed will vary.

To begin Centering Prayer, then, in a certain sense very little is required. As the psalmist would say, "Today, if you hear the voice of the Lord, harden not your heart." God's voice can be heard in the creation, in the voice of a friend, or in the more ecclesial ways of Scripture or liturgy. A person can practice Centering Prayer without a formal religious faith. A natural faith—if I can use such an expression—or knowing God through the creation, as Saint Paul says, is sufficient. Thus we can Center with those who are not Christians. We will talk more about this in a later chapter.

Essentially the Lord must be perceived in some way as knocking at the door and the door is opened. We open it because we desire. Perhaps those who cannot articulate precisely what they are seeking in opening the door are better off in some ways than those who have locked God into very sharply defined concepts. The person with a clear or elaborate conceptual theology or a rich imagery of what God should "look like" can miss God when the God of surprises shows up in another guise. "Eye has not seen, nor ear heard, nor has it entered into the mind of the human person."

When we begin to Center we will see ourselves more and more clearly in the eyes of the God who loves us. We will see more and more how we need to clean up our lives. We will grow in the desire to be ever more one with God. This leads to a deeper and deeper conversion, a real effort to eradicate from our lives not only all our deliberate sins but even those things which can lead us into sin. At the same time there will be a growing desire to search the Scriptures and to live the liturgical and sacramental life to the full in order to use every means we can to get to know God better and be more closely united to God. With this comes a greater desire to be one with the community of the faithful and the entire human family, and to reach out to others in their needs, whatever they be.

All of this can and does take place simultaneously with the regular practice of Centering Prayer. Such a complete conversion need not have taken place before one enters into the Prayer. For many it will never happen without the support and experience of the Prayer. If one is practicing Centering Prayer and there is no growth in these other dimensions of life, then the practice is to be questioned. We would have to ask ourselves whether we are truly seeking God in our practice or just deceiving ourselves and seeking ourselves in some way.

Regular practice of the Centering Prayer leads to an exquisite fidelity to Love. Like Christ, we come to seek to do only what pleases the Father. We are then ready to let all else go, holding all like him in a creative, caring Love.

There Is a Time and
a Place—and a Way

I f we have a real desire to share the gift the Lord has given us
and an openness to the Lord providing for us through
the events of life, we will find many opportunities to share
Centering Prayer.

"One-on-one" is certainly the most traditional way to share
this Prayer. The spiritual father or mother would have initi-
ated the disciple into it as soon as the appropriate opportunity
presented itself. A lay brother might have shared it with the
men who came along to help on the grange or with people at
the fair in the quiet lull after the noontime meal. Any intimate
moments with family, friend, or others might provide us with
an opportunity to share the Prayer. I find in traveling many
opportunities and even more fruitful ones in visiting the sick.
Many patients with time on their hands are buoyed up by a
sense that they can do something valuable for the whole world
and can escape from some of their boredom and pain. Why
not change what might just be so much idle chatter into an
occasion of grace? Even a serious encounter can be enriched,
grounded, and placed in a more loving and creative context by
the introduction of Centering Prayer.

Already *existing groups* of the faithful, especially in the
parish, can offer the place to share this gift. One of my students went home from our course with this in mind. First, she
went to her prayer group. They accepted it eagerly. When the
group members told others about their experience, other prayer
groups in the parish invited the student to come and share

with them. Then she went to the Single Women's Group and the Women's Guild; then to a younger counterpart of this, the Young Adults. She next went to the RENEW groups around the parish, especially those among the senior citizens in the high-rises. Before she had finished her rounds of the parish groups, invitations were coming in from larger diocesan groups. Another student, who was a member of his parish council, logically began there and with the support of the council brought the experience to all the other groups in his parish. Members have brought it back to the Knights of Columbus, Serra International, and the Holy Name Society.

We can step out and make more *general offers*. An offer in the parish bulletin might create an overwhelming response. One layman found himself standing before an audience of 450 in an overcrowded school hall after this offer was announced at all the Sunday Masses. A wonderful challenge! Retirement homes are a fruitful place to offer Centering Prayer and to form groups. Some have offered a Centering Prayer course as an elective in high school or CCD programs. Some have gone to Newman Centers, YMCAs (which are always looking for programs to offer), retreat houses and houses of prayer, and even to the local diocesan seminary. The seminarians were most appreciative. They liked the idea of learning about prayer from a laywoman. As we mentioned before, one even brought the Prayer to the city police force.

The establishment in a parish or school of a *meditation room* can be a real asset. It can always be there, inviting all to come apart and rest awhile. Set times for group meditations can be posted, with a brief instruction period for newcomers. Brief printed instructions can be left in the room for anyone to use at any time.

We need creativity and courage to bring into existence structures that will support us in doing what we really want to do.

Announcements or invitations, while concise, should give the prospective participants a clear idea of what to expect at the proposed session. Thus they can freely respond to a call of grace. Here is one good example:

Perhaps the time is right this Fall for a new prayer experience, one which is ancient but being rediscovered in our day. It is called Centering Prayer and it is simple, gentle, and nonthreatening. You won't have to "pray out loud" and there aren't any shoulds or oughts. Centering Prayer is rich, wonderful, and powerful.

Would you like to join us Thursday night?

Time: 7:30 p.m.

Place: Basement of the Church

Much of the sharing of Centering Prayer will be done in the informal one-on-one or in small group. The important thing is to adapt the sharing or teaching to the situation. We want to cover the essentials, but we don't need to share everything in the first meeting. How much we say will depend on the group's preparedness and the opportunities we may have to share further in later meetings.

One provincial opened a meeting with his counselors saying: "Why don't we pray a little differently today. Let's just settle down quietly, conscious of Jesus' presence in our hearts, and stay with him for a bit, gently repeating his name." That was enough for those men of prayer, even though they tended to be rather formal and would have had a lot of questions if they had been given a formal introduction. Many of them were surprised when they realized they had spent twenty minutes in prayer. They were also surprised how quickly they got through their agenda that day, all working together. Centering Prayer became a regular part of their meetings.

We want to remain always flexible and move with the Spirit. Each group and each opportunity will have its own grace. If an introduction to Centering Prayer is going to be given in a single formal session, I would suggest a format something like this:

- *Brief introduction*, giving the basic elements of the Prayer.

- *Centering* for twenty minutes.
- *Buzz session* of three to seven minutes, depending on the time. This helps get the sharing and questions started.
- *Break* of ten or fifteen minutes. Informal sharing.
- *Question period.* It might be good to have a couple of common questions to lead off, if necessary—e.g.: How do you pick the word? Do you stay with it? How do you know if you are doing it wrong? How often is it good to pray this way? What if you skip?
- Brief word on *lectio.*
- *Centering*—perhaps preceded by some physical exercise.
- Establish *follow-up.*

If one is asked to speak in a classroom, to preach a sermon, or to give a lecture not specifically billed as a Centering Prayer presentation, I think it is better not to try to teach the Prayer or lead people into the experience. It is better to talk about the Prayer, its tradition and its benefits, and then invite those interested to a learning session where they can have an experience of the Prayer. Such an arrangement ensures that only those who are hearing the invitation of the Lord to this deeper prayer are led into the experience. One person who is not comfortable with the Prayer can make the experience a negative one for everyone, with perhaps permanent loss for some.

If several sessions are going to be available for introducing the Prayer, it is well to consider the preparedness of the group. Some groups might benefit from an initial session on *lectio* with an intervening period to develop their faith and desire by this kind of contact with the Lord. (A brief summary of a simple method for *lectio* is given in the Appendix of this book. The method is described more fully in my book, *Lectio Divina*—see Bibliography.) The session might begin with the participants talking about their present prayer. This can be an affirming experience and offer the opportunity to hear about different kinds of prayer, opening the way to the desire for something more. The need for quiet to hear the Lord as the other Partner in prayer can be brought out, leading to the listening of *lectio*.

However, if the faith development of the group is such that they are ready, it is best to get right into Centering Prayer so that the group can begin to have the experience and have as many group experiences as possible through the course. *Lectio* and other supportive practices such as a rule of life and spiritual accompaniment (found in *Daily We Touch Him*, Chapter Seven and the Epilogue and in the Appendixes at the end of this book) can be brought out as the course proceeds.

In a full course, after the introductory session giving the basics along the lines of the single session described above, each session could have

- "A *Word from our Sponsor*"—a Scripture text that opens up the desire to Center. Some possible texts are John 14:23–27, 1:9–14, 1:35–39, 12:1–11; Matthew 11:28–30; Psalm 23[22]; Romans 10:17; 1 Corinthians 2:5–16; Song of Songs 5:2–7; Ephesians 3:16–19; 2 Peter 1:12–18; 1 John 4:7–21.
- *Centering*
- *Sharing and questions*
- *Input*: For this part various chapters of *Daily We Touch Him*, of *Centering Prayer*, and of this book could be used, as well as tapes from "A Centered Life" (see Audiocassettes in the Bibliography). Additional subjects might include *The Cloud of Unknowing*, Centering Prayer and the Sacraments, the challenge of other traditions, and the witness of men like Mr. Ferdinand Mahfood, Deacon Carl Shelton, and Cardinal Bernardin. Some groups may profit from basic catechetical instruction.
- *Centering*, preceded by some physical exercise.

A course of several sessions, say through the weeks of Advent or Lent, may very well evolve into an ongoing group that meets weekly.

The question has been asked about the use of some quiet background music during the time of Centering, especially if the meeting place is one that tends to be blessed with noises from the street or the like. Personally, I think it is best not to use such music. It is, in fact, only one more thing we can get caught up in and have to leave behind. Moreover, if we have such music during the introductory experiences, some are apt to think it necessary or become dependent on it and may not be able to practice the Prayer without it. That would be very limiting.

In all of this I would like to underline two things: dependence on Holy Spirit—in the teaching and sharing, in finding the opportunities, and in the format—and simplicity. K.I.S.S.

A Checklist for Sharers
and Teachers

Following is a proposed checklist for effectively sharing or teaching Centering Prayer. These are elements which I think we should keep in mind when we are sharing Centering Prayer with others.

CHECKLIST

Basic Principles
    Freedom
    Simplicity
    Aim
Teaching
    Posture
    Time
    Three Rules or Guidelines
    Experience
    Frequency and Regularity
Follow-up

Basic Principles

Freedom

Centering Prayer is certainly not the only way to pray nor the only way to enter into contemplative prayer. There are many effective methods to be found in our long, rich heritage. So Centering will not be everyone's way.

Some temperaments will find a contemplative type of prayer more difficult, at least initially. However, there are exceptions to every generality. I am sure that with God's call and grace no temperament will be a permanent obstacle to contemplative prayer. Contemplative prayer takes place at a level deeper than personality types.

For some, the time may not be right. The introduction may come at a time in our life when we are finding it extremely difficult to believe that God loves us or that we love him. It may be a time for more *lectio*, letting the Lord speak to us of his love through the gospels, especially the Last Supper discourse.

Although men and women and children seem to be entering into Centering Prayer at all ages, the Prayer might prove to be a special challenge for the adolescent. There is sometimes a great deal of confusion in life during that period of development, a lot of centering on self; feelings are very much to the fore. Undoubtedly, the practice of Centering Prayer could be a very helpful and stabilizing factor, especially if the young person has already established a steady practice and has persevered in it. But it might be a difficult time to begin. Yet it is often the time when young persons are looking for elements from an established past to help ground their own lives. Centering Prayer should be offered to adolescents with great gentleness, and openness and real personal support, yet granting them the freedom to not respond without guilt. The teacher should also be watchful that the adolescent does not latch on to Centering as a way to withdraw from worship and community.

Charismatics in the period of their initial experience are not in the space for Centering Prayer. It is usually a time of great emotional activity. As the charismatic experience matures—and this seems to be true of groups as well as individuals—there is usually an inclination toward more and more silent prayer. An established charismatic group would serve its members well if it provided an opportunity for them to learn Centering Prayer when they are ready. This could be one of the small-group possibilities available after the general meeting. Both

forms of prayer are totally dependent on the activity of Holy
Spirit.

Sometimes people feel too upset or angry with the Lord
for any prayer at all. Yet pray we must, for prayer is the very
breath of the human spirit. A silent, restful prayer, like Centering—just letting go and being and allowing the Lord's love to
seep in—is perhaps the best way to pray in such a period. The
House of Affirmation, a very successful therapeutic center for
clergy and religious, found Centering Prayer very helpful in
such cases. Obviously, it needs to be offered with great gentleness. In an institutional situation it might be best to make Centering Prayer available as a group experience which anyone
can freely and quietly join.

Saying that Centering Prayer is not necessarily the prayer
for all, I do not in any way imply that not all are called to an
intimate union with God. Such a union is offered to everyone.
The invitation is *always* there. But there are other ways to
respond to it. My mother entered into a quiet contemplative
prayer through the rosary, as have many others. Some
charismatics, especially those in leadership roles who must keep
the meeting going, have found that a deep, contemplative union
with God has developed beneath the praying and singing in
tongues.

It is not, however, a random happening that someone comes
into the space where Centering Prayer is being offered. God's
grace is at work. It is some sort of an invitation. All should be
encouraged to use the opportunity to learn the Prayer method
and give it a serious try in their lives if they can. They may
discover new spaces in life for it. Or it may be something for a
future day. Or it may be given to hand on to others or just as
an opportunity to understand better what others are experiencing.

It is important, then, in every sharing to place the invitation with delicacy and the fullest possible respect for the freedom of the other to accept the invitation or to pass it by at that
time.

Simplicity

Share the basic information as briefly and simply as possible. Try to get into the experience before any questions are asked or answered. The experience will answer most questions and those that are asked will come out of reality and not out of preconceived theory. We do not want to load people down with a lot of information that might prove our knowledge but just be a burden to them, and perhaps inhibit their simple entrance into the Prayer as experience.

It is a big challenge to keep it simple. We can easily fall into the trap of giving more, whether to prove our competence or just to enjoy the adulation that comes to the knowledgeable teacher. Let us be the humble, translucent servants of the Spirit, the only one who can really teach prayer. It is not only the teacher, however, who is challenged by simplicity; the learner will constantly wonder and even say aloud: There must be more to it than this.

Remember the story of Naaman the Leper. He had made a long journey. He had idolized the prophet. He had fancied just exactly how his cure should take place. Then all the prophet told him to do was go jump in a muddy old river. It was humble servants who had to convince him to do the simple thing, the only thing that would work. Some people have made a long journey in prayer before they first meet Centering Prayer. Not infrequently people idolize contemplative prayer and project some fantastic images upon it. We are all prone to imagine some of the remarkable things God will do to us in the contemplative states. To be told just to sit there and be gift—well, that is not quite the way it showed up in the lives of the saints, or was it? "Unless you become as a little child you will not enter into the Kingdom."

Aim

Always keep it very clear that the aim of Centering Prayer is not the practice. It is not to perfect the method, to do it right. The aim is one and only one. It is God—union with God. We may amplify this aim and put it in context but we must take care not to obscure it or let the accompanying benefits, rich though they be, overshadow the real meaning of what we are about. It is PRAYER. Anything else is accidental to that Reality.

Teaching

Posture

We must take care not to give posture undue importance and, again, allow for the greatest possible freedom. Yet posture does have its importance and its sacramental significance. Poor posture can hinder the freedom and restfulness of the Prayer. So it is good to say a few brief words about it: comfortable, back straight, eyes gently closed.

Many are helped by a bit of exercise just before Centering. This not only relaxes the body but also opens space. We are quickly taken up with exercises, leaving behind other thoughts and concerns. Yet when the exercises are over they do not tend to hold our mind. Thus a space is opened.

We should not, however, try to build certain exercises into the method itself and burden people with some sort of ritual. In teaching, it can be useful to describe a few exercises and even demonstrate some that have been found helpful. But it should be clear that these are only suggestions and are in no way part of the method. For this reason, when I am teaching I prefer never to do exercises before the first experience, so that the Prayer is fully experienced before any consideration of exercise. If the program is a longer one, comprising many actual sessions of Centering Prayer, I will take care to begin only some periods of Centering with exercises and have others without. This not only makes it clear that the exercise is peripheral, but also gives the participants an opportunity to learn by experience to what extent a warm-up exercise might benefit them.

Time

For beginners, we recommend habitually a period of twenty minutes. I would be hesitant ever to reduce this in a group. Individuals will find their own time under the Spirit. In general, however, twenty minutes should be recommended as a minimum for all.

Why is this? Almost everyone needs at least this amount of time to have a good, refreshing experience. To cut the time down risks depriving the pray-er of a good experience. If the first experiences are not good, the hope for perseverance is not high.

Moreover, a willingness to cut back on the time cannot help but create some false impressions. First of all, the impression can be given that it is difficult to spend twenty minutes quietly sitting with someone you love. If we convey the idea that it is supposed to be difficult, then more than likely the beginner will experience it as difficult. In fact, who of us has a real difficulty sitting twenty minutes with a good friend?

A willingness readily to cut back on the time can also give the impression that the Prayer is not important—one can easily minimize it; it is not really worth twenty minutes of our precious time.

Undoubtedly, beginners will at times express difficulty with the length, especially if their prayer life up to this time has been restricted to very short spurts or if they are leading hyperactive lives. It is, of course, people like this who most need to learn to slow down and give themselves and God a chance. I think a little tough love is called for here. I have found masters in other traditions rather inflexible in their demands as to duration. If you have been to charismatic prayer meetings or *cursillos*, you have experienced their tendency to throw the watch out the window and give God all the time God wants. Alleluia!

In groups, if the plaints of particular members are allowed to alter the duration of the Prayer, the leader will soon find that this will become a major concern and even a divisive factor. It should simply be taken as a given that the Prayer will last twenty minutes. If one or more of the participants want to pray with the group but feel unable to Center for twenty minutes, let them first examine why and see what they can learn from this. Then, if the matter cannot be remedied, let them Center as they can and then change over to some other form of silent prayer while the group continues to Center.

Three Rules or Guidelines

The helpfulness of the Centering Prayer method lies very much in its simplicity and clarity. However, the method works not of itself but because it opens space for God to work in us. There should be a certain suppleness in presenting the Rules or Guidelines. Father Thomas Keating tends to present them as four, incorporating in them some of what I present as preliminary matter. "Where the Spirit is, there is freedom." Christian prayer depends on the Spirit, not on any method.

Nevertheless, I think it is very important that learners have the Rules or Guidelines (as we have reformulated them in Chapter Four or as Father Thomas presents them) clearly in hand to take home with them to guide them as they begin the Prayer on their own.

I think it is also important always to ground the teaching in the Sacred Scriptures, even when time is very limited or the sharing is very informal. We may just remind our friends that Jesus promised at the Last Supper that he and the Father would come and dwell in us. In the Centering we are but responding to this promise and Reality. In more formal and spacious teaching opportunities we can always begin with "A Word from Our Sponsor."

Experience

Unless it is absolutely impossible, we should never share Centering Prayer with anyone without leading the participants into their first experience of it. It is an experiential prayer. The teaching will mean nothing until the experience is had. If the situation is such that we will absolutely have to leave them alone with Holy Spirit for their initial experience, well, so be it. It is better to teach it without the experience than not to share it at all. But it is far better to keep the explanation to a bare-bones minimum and get into the experience than to multiply the explanation and miss out on the experience.

Frequency and Regularity

We want to encourage very strongly two periods of Centering Prayer each day. All the great traditions urge morning and evening meditation. Today, however, some people's lives do run by different clocks, not related to natural sun time but to the demands of a technological society. Still, two periods enlivening roughly equal portions of their waking hours will be good. The aim of the Prayer as method is not just to open some good space twice a day for God. The aim is a totally Centered life. It is very clear from experience that this comes about much, much more quickly when the person Centers twice a day. It is a lot to expect sixteen hours of activity to flow steadily from the Center with only a twenty-minute meditation (or even a longer one) in the early morning.

The second meditation later in the day seems to have a special value. It is precisely what makes it most difficult—it has to be a quiet pool set into a busy, flowing stream—that gives it its special value. We stop and let go and really accept the primacy of God, that all we are doing is for God and that God can get it done without us if God wants. The main thing the Lord wants us to do with this precious gift of life is to learn how to love God and to receive God's gratuitous love. We also give a powerful witness to others when we take time out for prayer. This witness is most effective when we invite them to sit with us in the silence.

The Little Prince was told that he loved his little rose so much precisely because he had sacrificed so much for it. This is generally true: the more we sacrifice for something, the more we appreciate it.

Certainly, one of the things that will greatly support us in making time for two daily meditations is regularity. Most of us do have a regular rhythm we follow when we begin each day. Giving Centering Prayer its place in that rhythm ensures that our first meditation will find its natural place in our daily activity.

The second period also needs to be anchored, perhaps within the ending of the work day or the pre-supper rituals. For some, a time slot in their appointment book is the practical way to do this.

Whenever or however we do it, once we find what for us is the most natural way to situate these two Centering periods in our lives we will want to make them a regular part of our daily rhythm.

So, twenty minutes twice a day at a regular time and place.

Follow-Up

Follow-up is so important that I would now like to devote an entire chapter to consideration of it.

Follow-Up

Centering Prayer is a beautiful gift. When one is first exposed to it, this is usually a moment of invitation. The Lord is inviting his friend to a new and deeper union with him, a fuller and richer life, a closer bond with others—a Centered Life. But this transformation does not happen the first time one sits down to Center—at least not ordinarily. The Lord is the master of his gifts. Usually, it is a gradual process. The Lord respects the *humanity* he has given us, and this is the human way relationships grow and consciousness evolves.

So it is important, when we have the privilege of being the agents of God's invitation, that we also be the loving friend who helps a sister or brother to respond to the invitation. The flow of our quite frenetic world, the fascination of trifles, the habitudes of a lifetime militate against the beginner when he or she tries to make regular periods of Centering a part of life. The support of others who share the value and know the struggle to make time and place is for most an absolute necessity. Every successful movement or program for transformation has seen this and provided for it, whether it be something as "supernatural" as the charismatic movement of Holy Spirit or programs like Transcendental Meditation or Alcoholics Anonymous. (Certainly grace is working in these movements also. Wherever anything good is being accomplished by human action it involves God's grace. Nothing good comes from us as ultimate source.)

There is usually also a need for further input. This is probably the thing that most undermines a beginner's fidelity—the questioning. It is natural. The terrain is new and unfamiliar.

179

We are not sure. We need someone with whom we can talk. Even if that someone does not have the answers, a fellow traveler in the dark is a great support and consolation. Together we can read, seek out the sources of information, sit together listening to the Lord in our *lectio*, and share what we hear.

If we are teaching a course on Centering Prayer, a certain amount of immediate follow-up is built right into the course. Repeated Centering and ample space for questions to surface, along with the spontaneous sharing among the participants, all support the establishment of a firm and fruitful practice.

Even in the shortest or most informal of presentations it is good to try to say a word about the following accompaniments. In a longer program they can be developed at length, to the great profit of the learners.

Lectio

Centering Prayer flows out of faith, and that faith needs to be fed by hearing the Lord, hearing him in his gospels. The conceptual and affective levels of our prayer life also need to be fed so that they grow with the experiential. This creates a context in which we can articulate our experience and enable it to flow effectively into our lives.

Rule of Life

A personal and personally prepared rule of life is a most effective instrument to support us in regular practice of the Prayer. It is also a source of great joy, giving us a sense of taking charge of our life as we see it move in the direction we want. A practical method for formulating one's own personal Rule of Life can be found in the Appendixes of this book.

Spiritual Companion

These days it may be difficult to find someone to serve us as a spiritual father or mother, but we can readily offer someone the gift and grace of walking with us on the spiritual journey. Only openness and compassion are essential, though prudence, learning and experience would be real assets.

If Centering Prayer is introduced to an already existing group, the group itself provides the natural context for follow-up. Successive meetings should allow time for Centering. The space for sharing will naturally be present in or around the regular meetings. The teacher should obviously encourage this and offer effective suggestions.

Whenever we have the privilege of introducing a fellow pilgrim to Centering Prayer, several ways of providing some follow-up are available to us. One of these is *handouts*.

We might ourselves type up a brief explanation of Centering Prayer and have it copied or printed. I have seen many attractive and well worked out presentations, sometimes printed on a small card, that can be conveniently fitted into a pocket. Or we might use someone else's brief introduction. Liguori Publications has twice introduced Centering Prayer on the cover of its parish bulletin sheets, which I have often used. I once found a good half-page explanation of Centering Prayer by a young convert in the *Maine Catholic World*. Dove Publications of the Pecos Benedictines (Pecos, NM 87552) published a leaflet (#61) on Centering Prayer written by a permanent deacon, Robert O'Rourke. It is quite well done.

It is good to keep a couple of handouts in your pocket or your purse. You never know when in your daily travels you might have the opportunity to share the gift. At least you will have this follow-up to offer.

Books and tapes can amplify this sort of follow-up. If you are able to afford it, you might keep some copies to lend out to those you introduce to the Prayer. If you are teaching a course or offering the teaching publicly, you might want to have a supply on hand that the participants can purchase.

You could list a couple of the most useful sources on your handout and a place where they can be obtained. Centering Prayer resources can always be ordered from the Cistercian Book Service, Saint Joseph's Abbey (Spencer, MA 01562).

The most useful sources for a beginner would be *Finding Grace at the Center*, *Daily We Touch Him*, and *Centering Prayer*, and the cassette program "A Centered Life." *The Cloud of Unknowing* (Doubleday Image Books has a good edition prepared by Father William Johnston) will be more helpful after one has had some experience. A selective bibliography of material on Centering Prayer can be found at the end of this volume.

Personal *availability* is one of the best ways to support another who is learning to Center. A willingness to meet with the beginner to Center together and to talk over experiences and look at the questions that are arising is certainly a real service and outreach in Christlike love. Even when such meetings are impossible, the willingness to be available by telephone can be very supportive. Such availability says that we believe this Centering Prayer is important and that we really care for our friend and want to help him or her to enrich life with this gift.

You might consider putting your telephone number on your handout, offering such support as you can give.

Regular meetings are the normal and perhaps the best means of mutual support in Centering Prayer. Father Thomas Keating expresses a real reluctance to teach Centering Prayer if it is not possible to organize some sort of follow-up, and in particular Centering Prayer groups. Contemplative Outreach seeks to provide and support this.

Personally, I believe there is a value in sowing, making space for God himself to provide the watering and give the increase if that is all that is possible. We do what we can. But it certainly is much better to organize some practical follow-up.

When those who are beginning to practice Centering Prayer can meet regularly with their teacher or others who are Centering, such meetings do more than offer an opportunity for group Centering and getting some questions answered: they also establish a sort of gentle accountability. If we know we are going to meet in a week's time with our teacher or others, we have a certain incentive to be faithful to our practice and really give it a chance. We also sense throughout the week the support of the others who are each doing their Centering wherever they be. There is a sort of bonding, a sense of fellow travelers.

A follow-up meeting can best begin with some time for sharing, letting questions and difficulties emerge. There is space here for a lot of compassion and encouragement. Then the meeting moves to twenty minutes of Centering, with more time for sharing and questions after this experience. Some input can then be given. Some groups have listened to the different tapes available and discussed them. Finally, another period of Centering and some socializing can fill out the evening.

Such follow-ups quite naturally lead to the formation of an ongoing Centering Prayer group. We will speak of this in the next chapter. But before going on to that I would like to say a word about special times of vulnerability.

A lack of support, a lack of connection with others who share our values, leaves us very vulnerable. When we share the gift with others we should try to impress on them the importance of finding or creating support. It is their responsibility if they prize the gift and do not want to lose it. But we, too, have the privilege of bringing the gift into another's life should sense some responsibility to reach out in support even when it is not sought. Some people are shy or preoccupied with many things. They need someone to reach out to them.

Bad experience, particularly in the first days of our practice, can undermine our perseverance. This is especially true if we do not know how to handle such experiences. What do I mean by "bad experience"?

Bad experience can occur on the physical level: headaches or tenseness. Sometimes this is taken care of if we take a little more time disposing ourselves for the Prayer. Some physical or stretching exercise can be helpful here. However, these maladies are often caused by trying too hard. If we strain to suppress thoughts and images, we will soon have a good headache. We need to remember the words of the author of *The Cloud of Unknowing*: "Be careful in this work and never strain your mind or imagination, for truly you will not succeed in this way. Leave these faculties alone." Relax. Let the thoughts and feelings and images flow.

We also need to give up any self-seeking quest for certain

effects. Such seeking is a cause of frustration and therefore of strain. If we are simply seeking God, we have him. We are happy and at peace.

Beginners sometimes see as bad experience the surfacing of painful memories from the past or the upsurge of the passions: anger, lust, and the like. We need to remember that all the thoughts and feelings and images that come up during the time of our Centering are in themselves good, if only we let God use them the way he wants. We remain faithful to the Third Rule. The thoughts, images and feelings are allowed to go their own way—and take with them the tension they have built up in our lives. This surfacing is a healing thing, a healing of the memories, so that we can really let go of the past and be fully free to live in the NOW and move peacefully into the eternal NOW of God.

There are really no bad experiences in Centering Prayer if we remain faithful to the practice and the Three Rules or Guidelines. This is not always easy, however simple it might seem. At times we can be very upset, and even upset with God. It takes faith and courage and persistence, and oftentimes some support, too, to continue and let the healing take place. It is obviously at such times as these that we most need our Centering and can be most helped by it. Some tough love on the part of a supporter can be a very great blessing.

Surprisingly enough, one of the most dangerous times for our practice is the time of vacation. Also, the time of sickness. We would not expect that to be the case. On these occasions we usually have more time and space. What could be more recreative than Centering, more healing than the deep rest of this Prayer? The danger seems to lie in our having stepped out of our usual routine, which safeguarded the time for the Prayer. It gets put off as we sleep late or travel, and soon it is lost. Unfortunately, it often ends up being not just a vacation from the Prayer but the end of it in our lives. When we get back to our routine we feel a certain guilt about having put it off during the time we were vacationing or sick. We do not have the reinforcement we had when first beginning. So the Prayer does not refind its niche—which is quickly filled with the things that piled up while we were away.

In this regard a Rule of Life is very helpful. (See the Appendix on this.) Not only does the rule stand to affirm the place and value of Centering in our daily life but it can help us get back when we have strayed or let down our guard. We always want, as a part of our rule of life, a monthly retreat day—a day set aside for taking inventory and refurbishing our rule. It is to be expected, then, that we will at times miss out on things and that we will restore them on the occasion of this monthly renewal. Thus the place of the Prayer will not be lost for very long. The monthly retreat day can also provide the opportunity to do some extra Centering, reinforcing our good experience of the Prayer. It might also include a meeting with our companion on the journey, whose sharing can help us get reestablished.

I have suggested in this chapter only a few ways in which we can help a beginner get rooted in the practice. I am sure you can think of many others. A bit of creativity here can produce remarkable fruit. But now let us take a look at what is probably the most powerful means of long-term follow-up—the "Centering Prayer Group."

Centering Prayer Groups

Many kinds of prayer groups are happily flourishing today on the parochial scene. Christians are looking for support in prayer and for the inspiration of faith sharing and they are finding it or creating it. There are charismatic groups, Bible-sharing groups, *Cursillo* groups, and many others. And there are Centering Prayer groups.

It is not always necessary to start a new group. I mentioned earlier how one woman brought Centering Prayer to all the existent groups in her cathedral parish. It is good to bring the contemplative dimension to any group. Charismatics are soon ready for silent prayer. Bible sharing coming out of the silence will be deeper and more insightful. The sharing at *Cursillo* groups will be more honest, open, and loving if it is preceded by some time together in the Center.

Centering Prayer can be brought to the whole parish. A pastor visited me from Connecticut. He told me that in his parish every weekday Mass ends with a period of Centering after Communion. It was his plan to rearrange the Sunday Mass schedule and have Masses only every two hours so that there would be space for Centering on Sunday, too. I know of a parish in New Orleans where every Mass, service, and meeting begins with a period of Centering.

Another priest shared with me how his parish was transformed by a practice he started during Lent several years ago. Actually, he did it in order to help himself to be more faithful to Centering Prayer. He had no trouble with the morning period. But too often the afternoon one got squeezed out or he let it get squeezed out. So with the coming of Lent he posted a

notice for the parish: he would be in church every afternoon
from five until five-thirty Centering and everyone in the parish
was invited to come and join him in the church or join him
from wherever they happened to be. This did succeed in estab-
lishing his fidelity. If he was going to miss he had to post a
notice and explain why he would not be there. Everyone now
knew when it was time for Centering and would not detain
Father at that time. Anyone with him would be invited over to
the church to Center. But besides helping Father, this regular
period of Centering did a lot more. People were deeply moved
that their pastor was taking prayer so seriously. They were
encouraged to do likewise. Many asked for instruction in Centering Prayer. The parish began to have a conscious sense of
being together in prayer. When parishioners felt troubled or
alone they knew that at five they could go to the church and
find others to pray with them. The mother caught at home
with children and supper preparation could still be there in
spirit with the rest. Those sick abed knew the same experience. The parish, it seemed for the first time, consciously prayed
together. Needless to say, by common consensus the practice
was continued after Lent. And it has been carried to other
parishes.

These are not what might be called specifically Centering
Prayer Groups. They are rather Centered parishes—something
far better than groups.

The most fundamental group, and therefore the most natural group to pray together, is the family, the couple. It is an oft
told story, but each time I hear it I am deeply moved. Couples
tell me how Centering together opened new spaces in their life
together, a new freedom to be to each other in love. One wife
said recently:

> Prayer is the most intimate area a married couple
> shares....Our experience, as well as that of other
> couples, tells me prayer for a couple is more intimate
> than sex. When a couple enters into a commitment to
> grow together in prayer, the process becomes pretty

serious. The outcome is going to be a certain kind of continuing nakedness in front of each other. When we are talking even about something important, there are parts of ourselves we can hold back. But praying together is like taking a step into a mystery in which you can no longer say "I am going to hold back or give myself only in bits and pieces." That doesn't mean a married couple who pray together know everything about each other but if they continue, they will become more and more—well, naked is probably the best word to describe it.

Her husband continued:

Couple prayer has helped us to become aware of something we didn't understand early in our marriage: that when we were married, something new was created: our married relationship. Couple prayer comes out of the new creation. The uniqueness of this new creation in relationship to God is a reality, even though we do not fully understand it.

I have already reported some family experiences. Centering Prayer may not be the way for every family to sit together in prayer or for a family to do all the time. But it is worth trying. Times of silence together can be very healing and can help the younger members to discover a value so lost in our current American society.

Even with Centering going on in the home and in the parish church and in other groups one belongs to, I still find many who very much do want a specific Centering Prayer Group. They find such a group a great help to fidelity and regularity. It gives them a chance to clear up questions and to share with others on the same or on a similar path. It offers the opportunity to bring friends and introduce them to Centering. Especially is this helpful when one is shy about trying to teach the Prayer.

Each group can originate its own format. A common one is to begin with a period, really before the formal meeting, when new members are instructed in the Prayer. Members are constantly encouraged to bring friends. The meeting then begins with a period of Centering in which the new members can participate. There is time for questions and sharing after the Prayer. Some groups then have some input from a tape or a book. Others prefer to turn to *lectio* and share the next Sunday's gospel.

It is good, with such groups, to have a fixed schedule for moving along and concluding. Members can, of course, linger on, perhaps over refreshments, after the formal meeting is concluded.

A group does best if it has a stable leader or leadership team. That does not mean that in the actual meeting the different members cannot take turns leading the Prayer. Such alternation is good. The leader of the Prayer will open it with a brief expression of the movement in faith and love, coming into the Presence. At the end of the twenty minutes, she or he will pray the Our Father aloud at the same ample pace developed in daily Centering. The rest will follow these prayers interiorly with great freedom. Other concluding prayers can be used if appropriate, such as the *Gloria* (Glory to God in the highest), the *De profundis* (Ps 128[129]) or the *Magnificat*. It is best that the prayer be one that is common and can be said from the heart. It could be a spontaneous prayer. But K.I.S.S.

An established group can support the practice of the members in ways other than the weekly meeting:

- They can plan full *days of recollection* or *retreats* where they can do more Centering and sharing on Centering Prayer and Scripture.
- They can invite *teachers* to talk to the group and work with the members.
- A group might send one or more of its members to special *workshops* or *courses* for further training so that the fruit of the experience can be brought back to the whole group in oral reports and on tape.

- A *library* might be established, lending out to the members books and tapes and videocassettes on Centering Prayer and related subjects.
- A group might set up a *poustinia* or a retreat place for the use of the membership.
- A *meditation room* might be set up.

As a group matures it will probably find the charity of Christ compelling it to think in terms of some sort of corporate outreach. There are many possibilities here. Just to suggest a few:

- A group might decide to set up a *soup kitchen* or help out at an already existing one or at a Catholic Worker house.
- They might visit a *retirement home* and possibly teach Centering Prayer there.
- They might establish a *food* and/or *clothes closet* for the local poor.
- The group could *adopt* a child in the Third World or a seminarian.
- The members could *write letters* for Bread for the World, Amnesty International, and similar groups.
- They could promote, develop, and present *conscience-raising programs* related to hunger and social justice.

I believe that a group's prayer—just like an individual's prayer—that does not lead to outreach, according to the proper vocations of the members, is suspect. It has been a question in my mind—and I have shared it with them—why Catholic charismatics are almost wholly of the middle and upper middle class, while other charismatics have done much to share their grace and joy with the poorest of the poor in storefronts and the like. The Church, following her Master and Founder, has strongly expressed an option for the poor. If we do not share in that option, we need to ask ourselves: Why? I am happy to be able to say that there are Centering Prayer Groups among the poorest in inner city and minority groups. Catholic Workers have been prominent in sharing Centering Prayer. It has been taught in soup kitchens and drop-in centers and shelters, supporting the ministers in their difficult work and forming a bond with the guests. Yet I—for one—would like to see a great deal more done in this direction. It is undoubtedly difficult for the unemployed man or unwed mother or anyone else who is struggling for the most basic essentials of life and has to live in crowded, unstable environments to find the space and the will for such prayer. Yet who more needs the constant experience of God's caring love which affirms their true worth and dignity?

Centering Prayer Groups will then be reaching in and reaching out. But the group will need to take care that proposals for outreach do not become divisive. Even those who are closely united in love and prayer can see differently on social and political issues. We do in a Cistercian monastery. The American bishops do in their conference and leadership role. So can any other group of the faithful. A difference of opinion on particular questions which are open to different opinions does not mean a split. It is a call for greater mutual respect and love. When taking group action it is important to be sure that the minority does have its say. Consensus is the ideal to be striven after. Particular actions will have to be set aside at times as unripe, needing more prayer and reflection. After a difficult discussion, go back quickly to the Center and experience the deep, essential oneness in God.

It is probably best if Centering Prayer Groups are not allowed to become too large, though I have received reports of as many as twelve hundred meeting to Center together. It must be a very powerful meeting. New and especially young leadership can constantly be called forth. We give the young all too little opportunity to use their gifts and talents and make the contribution they want to make in the Church. Maybe that is why some of the best have gone to other groups that offer them more scope to make a difference with their lives. It would be good for a parish to have a group meeting every night of the week and some during the day.

One of my students proposed these "be-attitudes" to her group.

Be a pray-er.
Be punctual.
Be available to serve.
Be open.
Be hospitable.
Be present to others.
Be to God in faith and love.
Be-lieve that God delights in being with his people.

It does take these "be-attitudes" on the part of all, plus some dedicated leadership to make a Centering Prayer Group the powerful source of life and support that it can be. What a grace for a parish when it has even one such group. May you have the privilege of being God's instrument in bringing it into being and the joy of seeing its power and fruitfulness.

Beyond the Christian Community

C entering Prayer is a gift of our Christian heritage. It
comes to us from the earliest times and has always
found a place among us, albeit with different names
and manners of presentation.

Since it reaches back to the time of the undivided Church,
it is part of the common heritage shared by all the Christian
Churches. Ministers and lay persons from many communions
have sat with us in Centering and have taught the Prayer within
their own communities. For some, like the Society of Friends,
it comes as something very familiar. For others, it is a redis-
covery of something that had been largely lost.

For our Orthodox sisters and brothers the Prayer finds its
place within the tradition of the Jesus Prayer. Their tradition
centers on "Jesus" as the prayer word. Various methods of the
Jesus Prayer have evolved over the centuries, sometimes influ-
enced by other religious traditions. But where teaching is sim-
plest and purest, as for example in Russia and on the Holy
Mountain, it coincides with the teaching of Centering Prayer. I
have had the privilege of sharing Centering Prayer as the Jesus
Prayer with groups of Orthodox priests. I also have been invited by them to present it to their congregations. This has
always been an especially happy experience for me.

But what about seekers outside the Christian tradition?

First of all, what of our Jewish sisters and brothers?

There is a Rabbi, whom I have the privilege of calling a
friend, who has written extensively on Jewish mysticism and
spirituality and who seeks to live what he teaches. Last year I
asked him to read my book on Centering Prayer and tell me

what he thought of it as a Jew. I would like to share his response with you:

> Centering Prayer is not Jewish either in its technique or in its ethos—I was amused at the questions raising doubt about its Christocentric orientation; it couldn't be more Christocentric—and this in two ways: (1) In Jewish prayer, one brings oneself into the Presence of God but always through the simple meaning of the words of the liturgy. Just to be able to say, and mean it, "Adon Olam, Eternal God" or "Shma Yisrael, Hear O Israel" is the goal....There are certain strains of mystical Judaism which come closer to Centering Prayer but I can find no exact parallel. (2) As a Christian, you quite properly mix the existential reaffirmation (experienced in Presence) with love. You do it very well too and identify that as the distinctly Christian element in this technique. For a Jew though, God's love is only one of His attributes and we must try to be the object of the full range of His person. He is also angry, demanding, just, gracious, intellectual, moral, etc. The Jewish prayer life is, therefore, intended to bring us into the full range of the Presence. You may be intending to say this, but it is not immediately clear from the book. The emphasis on the centrality of love is truly Christian. Having said all that, I think, that, given a Jewish prayer word, ethos, and expectations, there is nothing to prevent a Jew from using the technique to great profit. It's not our way, but it would prove to be a useful way into God's complex Presence.

All religions go back to an earliest period of experience, from which they preserve memories and stories. The psalms command, "Tell it to your children." Jesus commanded, "Do this in memory of me." We tell the stories of Eden and Sinai, of Bethlehem and Calvary and the empty tomb. In those earliest days, holiness was everywhere. Abraham met his God here and there. Jesus said it would no longer be in Jerusalem or on Mount Garzim, but everywhere, that the Father would be worshiped in Spirit and in truth.

Only after the experience would the event be ritualized—the Passover Meal, the Mass—the ritual making the saving event present again for today. Institutions would grow up—the synagogue, the church—to preserve the memories and stories and conduct the rituals.

I was struck strongly by this one Holy Thursday in Rome. I was in the Basilica of St. John Lateran, the pope's own cathedral. The pope himself had celebrated the liturgy, ordaining twelve bishops. After the solemn rite, full of pomp and ritual, the altars were stripped. There, surrounded by the rich baroque marble that made it the papal altar, was the simple wooden table that tradition said Saint Peter used to celebrate the Lord's Supper in a private home in Rome. The simple table's rich encasement symbolized and summed up the whole evolution from those days when the first shepherd of the city fed his flock to the day when good Pope John, crowned with the triple crown, entered upon the shoulders of noblemen.

This evolution is so connatural to the human spirit that we see it taking place even within families as they create their own particular ways of celebrating birthdays and national feasts: Fourth of July, Thanksgiving gathering, etc.

But deep within us all there is always the desire to go through all this ritual and participate truly in the original experience. That is what Centering Prayer does on the religions plane. It takes us to the open space where the original experience of God took place. It takes us to the ground of all being, the Source of all being. In this regard, it answers to the deepest aspirations of all religious persons whatever their tradition, whatever was that first experience out of which grew their particular expression of faith.

We do need to return to this experience if our own religious faith is to be truly alive and not just a thing of ritual and story. And yet, although the desire to return is connatural to us, we are yet prone to get settled in the safety of ritual and not pierce through into the unknownness of the experience.

Jesus repeatedly inveighed against our tendency to seek safety in ritual and observance and miss the reality. In this he was just following his Father, from whom he derived all that he had. In the time of the prophet Ezekiel, God took from his people the temple which he himself had designed and the ritual his law had spelled out in detail. Then came the great vision of the prophet. He saw a human form, the greatest image of God, reverence for which God wanted above all else, and a moving chariot, an elaborate, awesome, transcendent ritual inviting the beholder to transcendence.

God never wanted to be enclosed in any image or ritual. He summoned Moses up into a cloud of unknowing. Moses was to "come up the mountain and be there." No beast or human was to approach. Moses was to leave all behind. He was to "be there." Not just there physically, but there with his whole being. In the end, when he did see God, he could only record the experience as having seen God after God had passed, for in the moment of the seeing Moses could only be to God and there would be at that moment no Moses to record the seeing.

Earlier Jacob had wrestled to see and know he had seen, but he did not see, because he was not willing to relinquish the "I": "God was in this place and I, the I, did not know it."

All must be left behind to see the living God. Elijah stood at the mouth of the cave and covered his face when the approach of the Lord was announced by the still, small voice. There was no Elijah there to record for us what he saw.

When the Jews wanted to circumscribe God, as had all their pagan neighbors, with a temple and a shrine, God reluctantly gave in to them, warning them of the possible consequences. But the shrine he gave them was unique and according to his own transcendent nature. Where the other nations carried forth the idol of their gods on a palanquin, the Jews carried on their shoulders only a sacred space surrounded by the hovering wings of two adoring cherubim.

This was the Center of Judaism, a space—space we can now find within in Spirit and truth. For the kingdom of God is within. We are the temples of God.

As the devout Jew comes to his prayers he hovers beneath his shawl and covers his face. To be in silence in the Presence of God is certainly not foreign to him. The Shma Yisrael might well give him his prayer word, his love word, for this God has ceaselessly and shamelessly proffered his undying love to Israel.

I am not very familiar with Islam. A more transcendent type of prayer seems to flourish among their Sufis. A disciple of a Persian *shake* (Sufi master) visited me. She readily identified Centering with one of their forms of meditation or prayer, as did Thomas Merton in his letter to a Sufi which we quoted in an earlier chapter. Certainly there is nothing incompatible with the tenets of Islam in going to God in this inner way.

Eastern religions have perhaps less in common with Christianity than Judaism and Islam, yet find it less difficult at times to accept our more contemplative ways. They will usually identify with them and draw parallels. For most Hindus, Jesus is just one of the many manifestations of the one God. They have no difficulty in worshiping him. Each person is entitled to have his or her own chosen deity or manifestation of God. Jesus is the manifestation for the West (Hindus sometimes offer him Coke and potato chips rather than rice and chapati when they perform the *puja* in his honor). It is difficult for the Hindu to understand why an Indian would choose Jesus: it seems disloyal to India; yet the devout Hindu is free to use all methods of worship and meditation.

One day a swami, who was a monk of the Ramakrishna order and also a medical doctor, took me to visit Mother Teresa's home for the dying in Benares, the sacred city on the Ganges. It was an unforgettably touching experience to find such light and joy surrounding so much suffering. As we were leaving, we met a group of professors and students from Benares Hindu University. When my guide introduced me as a teacher of Christian meditation, they immediately wanted to learn. The crowded home for the dying hardly offered space, so we set off down the street. A hospitable Jain priest cleared the garden of his temple, opened the shrine, and put it at our disposal. Here was a Christian monk teaching prayer to Hindu students in a Jain temple. They were delighted with the experience. What appealed to them most was the simplicity and effectiveness of the method. Their own swamis, depending on natural means, tend to offer quite complicated methods, as I have often experienced.

It is my sense, from having meditated with persons from many different traditions, that in the silence we experience a deep unity. When we go beyond the portals of the rational mind into the experience, there is only one God to be experienced. When we return we are forced, if we are to speak at all and communicate anything of our experience, to fall back on our own philosophical and theological concepts. We find ourselves saying different things—things almost, if not entirely, incomprehensible one to the other. But I wonder if we are not all attempting to speak about the same Incomprehensible One. Catholics have always taught the doctrine of "baptism of desire"—the fact that any person of good will who says "Yes" to the truth, however he or she perceives it, comes into grace. And it is the grace of Christ, for there is no other, whether it is recognized or not. By this baptism a real relationship is established with our one God who is Truth.

I am convinced that Centering Prayer can be practiced by any human person and can be real prayer for him or her even though the word "prayer" and its meaning may be foreign. This is why I have not hesitated to share Centering Prayer whenever the occasion has, in God's providence, presented itself.

Some years ago I had the privilege of inaugurating, with a group of dedicated bishops, priests, ministers, rabbis, and lay persons, an organization called the Mastery Foundation. The purpose of the foundation is "to wake the sleeping giants"— to call forth the great religious institutions which have within themselves enormous power to become agents of transformation. To this end, as our first endeavor, we have been offering to those whose lives are dedicated to sacred ministry in these institutions a course on how to make a difference. (Sad to say, we have found a very large number of men and women in sacred ministry who feel personally that their lives are not making a difference or are making very little difference.) The aim of this course is to enable the participant to open to a shift in consciousness, that shift expressing itself in Centering Prayer. The courses offered so far have been very successful. The fruits in the lives of the participants are significant. A good number of these men and women in ministry, after taking the course, have given many hours and gone to great expense to prepare themselves to lead the course for others. So far the participants have been largely from the Christian and Jewish communities, although a few have come from other religious traditions.

I have prepared a brief presentation of Centering Prayer as a handout for the Mastery in Ministry course. Here is the introduction:

CENTERING

A Brief Presentation for Those of Different Religious Traditions

Each of the great religious traditions has its own way of conceiving and speaking about the Ultimate Reality and our experience of him/her/it. In every tradition there is a quest for a certain realization of our oneness with that Reality, however that union may be conceived. The Christian tradition, with which the writer is most familiar, recalls the parting words of our Master, the Lord Jesus: "If anyone keeps my word, my Father and I will come to him and make our dwelling in him." "That they may be one in us, as you, Father, in me and I in you." Christians share in their Jewish brothers and sisters' realization of God as creator. Going to the Source of their being, Jews and Christians touch the Divine Creative Presence. Hindus are aware of a Divine Presence in all beings. Buddhists would express all of this differently, especially those who realize the need of going beyond all rational thought. Centering invites all on a spiritual path to sit in the silence, guided by their own proper principles of faith and understanding, seeking that ultimate experience toward which their particular path directs them. Jews and Christians and Others who know God as a Provident Lover will speak of Prayer, being aware of a communion of love in the silence. Philosophers and theologians discuss whether, when we pass beyond thoughts and concepts into the "experience," we all come into the same Reality or not, and whether the experience really differs or only our feeble efforts to conceptualize it. I think it has been the common experience of all persons of good will that when we sit together Centering we experience a solidarity that seems to cut through all our philosophical and theological differences.

In this context, I then present the Three Rules with very little modification. The result has been an almost universally gratifying experience.

I do not think, then, that our response to the Lord's command, "Freely have you received, freely give," needs to be limited to fellow Christians. I think we can share the gift of Centering Prayer with those of other traditions who are open to receive it. Many of these traditions have been very generous and open in sharing their tradition. Sometimes we give the impression of having nothing to offer. We do have a very rich and grace-filled tradition. We should—with humility, but with dignity and joy—share what we have.

Epilogue: A Centered Life

It is time to bring this sharing to a close. There is so much more I could put in this book—infinitely more. But it is time to let it go and make space for something else. I hope you are not disappointed with what you have found here—that you will find some of the chapters worth returning to more than once. And if this book leaves you still wanting more—that is good. There are other writers to whom you can turn. I especially recommend my spiritual father, Father Thomas Keating.

Writing this book has been a beautiful experience, yet frustrating, too. It has been a joy to gather up something of what I have learned and share it with you. It has been frustrating because I found myself at times trying to express the inexpressible. As I went along I often stopped for prayer, to Center, and for a word of Scripture. I have a very real sense that what I have written not only falls far short of the Reality but is indeed flat, conveying little of the tremendous excitement that this experience of God brings into life. However, I do not think my publisher is ready to accept pages and pages of "Alleluia!"

I am very conscious that I have not treated many important areas of the Christian life—and every one of them is profoundly affected by the regular practice of Centering Prayer. I think especially of the liturgical life and the sacraments. I am very aware that I have not written of Mary, the model and mother of a Centered Life. I will refer you to the last chapters in *Daily We Touch Him* and *Centering Prayer*. Mary certainly remains a very important person in my life, close to our Savior, a constant help and inspiration, to say the very least. I have no excuse for these omissions except my desire to avoid repetition and to keep this book from getting too long. There has been more than enough to share.

When it comes to speaking about something that is beyond our usual consciousness, transforming that consciousness and bringing us into unity-consciousness with God, it may be better to say less and let Holy Spirit take over. On the night before he died, our Master promised us he would send Holy Spirit who would teach us all things, calling to mind whatever Jesus had taught us. It was precisely at that time that Jesus told us about the indwelling and prayed that we might be one with him and the Father even as they are one with each other. That is what Centering Prayer and a Centered Life are all about.

When we open to Centering Prayer we open to the Spirit of Jesus and to her free operation in us through her gifts. These gifts include not only wisdom whereby we savor God and understanding, which enables us to find God in all—as Francis Thompson said so beautifully and simply:

Lo here
Lo there
Lo Christ
    is everywhere.

—and knowledge which enables us to find all in God. The Spirit also activates the gift of courage to act to create a Centered world, one that is re-created according to its original nature and beauty, and the gift of counsel to know how to go about doing our bit.

I was asked to write the introduction to a book of presentations on Thomas Merton. The book had an interesting title: *Getting It All Together*. I think Tom did that in the end or came very close to it. In his last week we find him going as a devout Christian pilgrim, with relics in his pocket, to the shrine of the apostle Thomas and then on to an enlightening experience walking barefoot in the moist grass at the great Buddhist shrine in Polonnaruwa. He was able to enjoy the jazz in the bars of Colombo and touch the poor and in penetrating talks and keen discussion challenge the consciences and consciousness of us all. He was openly in dialogue with all; he called upon monks and nuns to take seriously what he saw as the fundamental message of Karl Marx and to seek to create a just society where the bounty given freely by our common Father is the shared blessing of us all.

Even while a Centered Life carves out due time and leisure for God and self and knows a profound peace and joy, yet, in compassion, it weeps with those who mourn, hungers and thirsts for justice, exercises a generous mercy toward all and works tirelessly to bring to the world that peace which has been found within.

This is the vocation of every Christian; it is the way of the beatitudes. It is fundamental Christian life. Centering Prayer is a simple, powerful, efficacious way to come into freedom to live Christian life to the full.

If we have received this gift we want to treasure it, showing our gratitude by using it well and our love by sharing it widely. I feel there is a special urgency about this now. As we enter into the new millennium, we are called by God to participate in the creation of the new heaven and the new earth. We need all the creative love we can open ourselves to receive. Supporting our sisters and brothers in faith and hope, responding to their growing experienced desire for something more, is the mission of the Church in an age filled with hitherto unconceived and frightening potential. A powerfully Centered life will be our source of strength.

Yet, when we come to sharing Centering Prayer, let us always do it with the humility that reverences God's free work in others. The Lord leads us all, each in his or her own proper way.

There was once a holy bishop who was sailing through the South Seas. As the ship approached a small island, the crew told the bishop that three hermits lived there cut off from almost all human contact. The pastoral heart of the bishop reached out to his brothers. He asked the captain to stop the ship so one of the men could row him ashore to visit these hermits.

The bishop quickly found the three close to their little hut. He was edified by their poverty and simplicity. Their life seemed truly worthy of monks. As he blessed them and was about to take his leave he asked them to pray the Lord's Prayer with him. The three replied that they did not know the Lord's Prayer. The bishop was taken aback: "How do you pray?" The three lined up in front of their hut and began: "We are three." They raised their hands heavenward: "You are three. Have mercy on us and save us."

The bishop was shocked. He begged the sailor's leave to stay a bit longer and set about teaching the monks the Lord's Prayer. After more than a bit of time—for they were slow albeit willing learners—he had the joy of hearing them recite the Prayer with him. He blessed them and took his leave.

When he got back to the boat, the bishop sat in his room, pondering this experience—monks who did not even know the Lord's Prayer. Suddenly there was a pounding on his door. An excited sailor burst in and shouted that he must come to the deck at once. As he pushed through the crew, the bishop saw the cause of all the excitement. There, running swiftly across the water and just now catching up to the ship, were his three hermits. "Bishop, Bishop," they cried, "come back to us and teach us, for we have already forgotten the Lord's Prayer." "My sons," said the bishop, leaning over the rail, "go back in peace, and pray as you can, for the Lord God is your God."

As my first spiritual father often said, quoting Dom Chapman:

Pray as you can, don't pray as you can't.

If you have a loving relationship with God and a fruitful way of expressing and living it, then do not let anyone take that from you, be he bishop, beatus, or Basil.

Blessed be God in all his gifts!

Appendixes

Appendix One
Guidelines for Centering Prayer

S it comfortably in a chair that will give your back good
support and gently close your eyes. It is well to choose
a place where you will not be disturbed by any sudden
intrusion. A quiet place is helpful, though not essential.

THREE RULES OR GUIDELINES

Sit relaxed and quiet.

1. Be in faith and love to God who dwells in the center
   of your being.
2. Take up a love word and let it be gently present,
   supporting your being to God in faith-filled love.
3. Whenever you become aware of anything, simply,
   gently return to the Lord with the use of your prayer
   word.

Let the Our Father (or some other prayer) pray itself.

Centering Prayer lies within a living Christian tradition.
Even the name has evolved through the centuries from the early
Christians who called it the *monologion*, or "one-word" prayer.
It has been called Prayer of the Heart, Prayer in the Heart,
Prayer of Simplicity, Prayer of Simple Regard, etc. And the
presentation has been adapted to the people of each age. It is
not surprising then that in our times it finds different presenta-

tions, largely because of the audience that is being served. Thus we now find Father Thomas Keating presenting Centering Prayer in a slightly different form, summoning it up in four guidelines:

FATHER THOMAS KEATING'S FOUR GUIDELINES

1. Choose a sacred word as the symbol of your intention to consent to God's presence and action within.
2. Sitting comfortably and with eyes closed, settle briefly and silently introduce the sacred word as the symbol of your consent to god's presence and action within us.
3. When you become aware of thoughts return ever-so-gently to the sacred word.
4. At the end of the prayer period, remain in silence with eyes closed for a couple of minutes.

Appendix Two
Guidelines for *Lectio Divina*

It is well to keep the Sacred Scriptures enthroned in our home in a place of honor as a real Presence of the Word in our midst.

1. Take the Sacred Text with reverence, acknowledging God's Presence, and call upon Holy Spirit.
2. For five minutes (or longer if you are so drawn) listen to the Lord speaking to you through the Text and respond.
3. At the end of the time, choose a word or phrase (perhaps one will have been given to you) to take with you and thank the Lord for being with you and speaking to you.

Appendix Three
Guidelines for Preparing
a Rule of Life

First, we take some time to come into the presence of God and to seek the help and guidance of Holy Spirit. It is good to read something like 1 Corinthians 2, which we have cited in the Foreword, to help us realize how completely dependent we are on her in the discernment of questions that vitally effect our life and happiness as persons who have been baptized into Christ and share in his divine life and nature.

Then we take four sheets of paper.

On the first we seek to express as precisely and concisely as possible our goals in life, what we want to do with our lives, what we want to get out of life and put into it. This should be very realistic, listening deeply to our nature as man or woman, our Christ-nature, our vocation or charism, our gifts and talents. Satisfactorily responding to these, we have then to make what choices are necessary to concretize the goals of our journey so that we have something on which we can really set our sights.

On the second sheet of paper we seek to list as concisely yet completely as possible all that we need to do or acquire in order to attain our determined goals. We should be very concrete here, and practical. We should include the basic needs of our nature, such as sleep, food, friendship, work, study, etc.; the needs of our Christ-nature, such as that amount of prayer, sacred reading, etc., that we need to be satisfactorily responding to the Father; and then those things necessary to fulfill our vocation and all the other choices we have made.

As we come to the third sheet, we should prayerfully look back over a significant period of time, a few months to a year or so. Perhaps this could be the time since our last retreat, or since our life took a significant turn through graduation or a new job or something of that sort. Looking at this period we should try to perceive and note all the things in our life: situations, events, activities, our own passions or emotions, etc., which have been hindering us from attaining our goals.

Finally, on the fourth sheet—and this might be the most difficult part of the exercise—we formulate for ourselves a Rule or Program of Life, on a daily, weekly, and monthly cycle. With this we seek to assure that there is place in our life for all those things we need to do to attain our goals and to eliminate those things we experienced as obstacles. Since we cannot possibly fit into twenty-four days and seven-day weeks all that we want to do, we will here have to make some difficult choices, giving up good things in order to pursue the things that we really want.

Important in this Rule of Life is a monthly retreat day, or some other regular periodical "climbing up a high tree" to see where we are. This is important not only to see if we are actually following our rule of life. It is important so that we may experience, in a very conscious way, that happiness that comes from knowing we are actually moving along toward the attainment of our goals.

Select Bibliography

Books

Abishiktananda (Fr. Henri Le Saux, OSB). *Prayer* (Philadelphia: Westminister Press, 1973).

Benson, Herbert. *Relaxation Response* (New York: William Morrow, 1975).

____. *Beyond the Relaxation Response* (New York: Time Books, 1984).

Bloom, Anthony. *Beginning to Prayer* (New York: Paulist Press, 1971).

____. *Living Prayer* (Springfield, IL: Templegate, 1966).

Chatiton of Valamo. *The Art of Prayer* (London: Faber & Faber, 1966).

Dairymple, John. *Simple Prayer* (Wilmington, DE: Michael Glazier, 1984).

Evagrius Ponticus. *Praktikos Chapters on Prayer* (Spencer, MA: Cistercian Publications, 1970).

Griffiths, Bede. *Return to the Center* (Springfield, IL: Templegate, 1976).

Hausherr, Irénée. *The Name of Jesus* (Kalamazoo, MA: Cistercian Publications, 1978).

Higgins, John J. *Thomas Merton on Prayer* (Garden City, NY: Doubleday, 1972).

Hodgson, Phyllis, ed. *Deonise Hid Divinite and Other Treatises on Contemplative Prayer Related to The Cloud of Unknowing* (London: Oxford University Press, 1955).

John of the Cross. *The Collected Works* (Washington, DC: ICS Publications, 1973).

Johnston, William, ed. *The Cloud of Unknowing and the Book of Privy Counselling* (Garden City, NY: Doubleday, 1973).

Johnston, William. *The Inner Eye of Love* (San Francisco: Harper & Row, 1978).

_____. *The Mysticism of the Cloud of Unknowing* (St. Meinrad, MD: Abbey Press, 1975).

_____. *Silent Music* (New York: Harper & Row, 1974).

_____. *The Still Point* (New York: Fordham University Press, 1970).

Kadloubowsky, E. and G.E.H. Palmer, eds. *Early Fathers from the Philokalia* (London: Faber & Faber, 1954).

Keating, Thomas. *At the Heart of the World* (New York: Crossroad, 1982).

_____. *Intimacy With God* (New York: Crossroad, 1994).

_____. *Invitation to Love* (New York: Continuum, 1992).

_____. *Open Mind Open Heart* (Warwick, NY: Amity House, 1986).

Keating, Thomas, et al. *Finding Grace at the Center* (Still River, MA: St. Bede's Press, 1978).

Lawrence, Brother. *The Practice of the Presence of God* (Springfield, IL: Templegate, 1974).

Louf, Andre. *Teach Us to Pray* (New York: Paullst Press, 1978).

Maloney, George. *Inward Stillness* (Denville, NJ: Dimension Books, 1976).

Main, John. *Moment of Christ, The Path of Meditation* (London: Darton, Longman & Todd, 1984).

Merton, Thomas. *Contemplation in a World of Action* (Garden City, NY: Doubleday, 1973).

_____. *Contemplative Prayer* (Garden City, NY: Doubleday, 1971).

_____. *The New Man* (New York: Farrar, Straus & Giroux, 1961).

_____. *New Seeds of Contemplation* (New York: New Directions, 1961).

Pennington, M. Basil, *A Place Apart* (Liguori, MO: Liguori/Triumph, 1998).

_____. *Awake in the Spirit* (New York: Crossroad, 1993).

_____. *Call to the Center* (Hyde Park, NY: New City Press, 1995).

_____. *Centering Prayer* (Garden City, NY: Doubleday, 1980).

_____. *Challenges in Prayer* (Wilmington, DE: Michael Glazier, 1982).

_____. *Daily We Touch Him* (Kansas City, MO: Sheed & Ward, 1997).

_____. *Lectio Divina: Renewing the Ancient Practice of Praying the Scriptures* (New York: Crossroad, 1998).

_____. *Retreat With Thomas Merton* (New York: Continuum, 1988).

_____. *Thomas Merton, Brother Monk: The Quest for True Freedom* (New York: Continuum, 1997).

_____. *Thomas Merton, My Brother: His Journey Into Freedom, Compassion, and Final Integration* (Hyde Park, NY: New City Press, 1996).

Richards, M. C. *Centering in Pottery, Poetry and the Person* (Middletown, CT: Wesleyan University Press, 1964).
Teresa of Ávila. *Interior Castle* (Garden City, NY: Doubleday, 1961).
____.*The Way of Perfection* (Garden City, NY: Doubleday, 1964).
William of St. Thierry. *On Contemplating God, Prayer, Meditations* (Kalamazoo, MI: Cistercian Publications, 1977).

Audiocassettes

Keating, Thomas. "The Spiritual Journey" (Butler, NJ: Contemplative Outreach, 1988).
Meninger, William. "Contemplative Prayer" (Spencer, MA: St. Joseph's Abbey, 1975).
Pennington, M. Basil. "A Centered Life: A Practical Course on Centering Prayer" (Kansas City, MO: Credence Cassettes, 1981).
____."The Contemplative Attitude" (Kansas City, MO: Credence Cassettes, 1981).

Videocassettes

Keating, Thomas. "The Spiritual Journey" (Butler, NJ: Contemplative Outreach, 1988).
Pennington, M. Basil. "A Matter of Love" (Kansas City, MO: Credence Cassettes, 1984).
____. "How to Center Your Life" (Allen, TX: Argus Communications, 1985).

Internet Resources

Centering Prayer <centeringprayer.org>
Contemplative Outreach <centeringprayer.com>
"centeringprayer" dialogue list <onelist.com>
"Spiritus" dialogue list <maelstrom.St. Johns.edu>
"Center-L" dialogue list <maelstrom.St. Johns.edu>
Lectio Divina <http://www.osb.org/osb/gen/topics/lectio>
    www.lectiodivina.org